Let another praise you, and not your own mouth;
someone else, and not your own lips.
–PROVERBS 27:2

I have known Randall since my Orlando Renegade Football and Dixon Ticonderoga days and I truly value his friendship. I recall giving his daughter a yellow, six-foot-tall Dixon Ticonderoga pencil that thrilled her seventh grade First Academy students. Whenever I had a need from the city, I did not call the mayor—I called my friend Randall! His book, *Morphing Orlando . . . into a World-Class City*, will demonstrate how I got through "bureaucratic red tape."

—COACH LEE CORSO
ESPN COLLEGE FOOTBALL ANALYST

Randall and I both have served in the executive branches of government as well as Southern Baptist Convention pastors. I can confirm his behind-the-scenes look at serving his country and his Lord require a bold yet humble balance. *Morphing Orlando . . . into a World-Class City* will give many a greater appreciation of both.

—GOVERNOR MIKE HUCKABEE

Randall is one of the most generous, caring, and thoughtful persons I have ever known. He is loved by people across racial, cultural, class, gender, and denominational lines. I've told people that if he decided to run for mayor of Orlando, he would win by a landslide.

—DR. JAMES B. HENRY
FIRST BAPTIST ORLANDO PASTOR EMERITUS

Pastor Randall James—how blessed I am to have had him in my life for so many years as an example of a loving, born-again Christian who not only talks the talk, but walks the walk. I smile that he is my friend, and I laugh because there is nothing he can do about it! We truly will be friends forever—just wait and see!

—GRACE ANN CHEWNING
ORLANDO CITY CLERK EMERITUS

I have had the privilege of knowing Randall since he became an Orlando police officer and served with my dad. I have watched him firsthand effectively serving in the executive branch of government and then as an under shepherd of his church. His book is an inspirational read and I am proud to call him friend.

—CHIEF JUDGE BELVIN PERRY
NINTH JUDICIAL CIRCUIT OF FLORIDA

It has been my joy to have spent over seven years serving side by side with a man I have grown to love and appreciate. I have never served with anyone who has greater favor with God and man. My journey is richer today because I got to work alongside Randall James. Pastor Randall's book will open the eyes of many to the intricacies of always putting Christ first while serving mankind.

—DR. DAVID UTH
FIRST BAPTIST ORLANDO SENIOR PASTOR

After reading *Morphing Orlando...into a World-Class City*, my mind was flooded with many similar memories—some great, some not so great! Like Randall, I, too, worked in the Orlando mayor's office (Mayor Langford) and I have served as Orlando's Police Chief. This book will give you a clear picture of government infrastructure and how to integrate your faith in getting the job done.

I have known Pastor Randall for over a decade and have watched him successfully chair the Southern Baptist Convention's Executive Committee. I have heard testimonies of how he helped lead a growing metro area where my wife and I always enjoy visiting. After reading his educational book, I think it is safe to ask the question, "Who said you can't mix politics and religion?"

In 1980, I met Randall when I was first elected to the Florida legislature and have enjoyed working with him on issues to enhance the quality of living in Central Florida. He is my brother in Christ and I know of his boldness in using cancer as a platform to encourage others and to share the gospel of Jesus Christ. His book will demonstrate how to get it done in government as well as in the church.

I have known Pastor Randall James for several years. During that time, I have had the opportunity to watch a true Christian man interact with others and myself. He is one of the kindest persons I have ever known. His slow, southern drawl washes all over those who hear him speak. The Lord has used him for so many years in so many ways, first as a young man, then as a husband, father, and grandfather, and finally in several key positions in the development of the Orlando area, much of the time while battling cancer. For several years, he has been encouraged by others to write a book. What you hold in your hand is a product of a "Normandy miracle." As you read, you will understand the meaning of that last phrase. It has been my pleasure and delight to know more about RJ as he wrote this book. It is my hope, and his, that your life will be changed by reading this book.

—PAT BIRKHEAD
AUTHOR AND EDITOR

Governor Huckabee and Congressman Webster

Dr. Frank Page

Morphing
Orlando
into a World-Class City

RANDALL JAMES

CREATION
HOUSE

MORPHING ORLANDO by Randall James
Published by Creation House
A Charisma Media Company
600 Rinehart Road
Lake Mary, Florida 32746
www.charismamedia.com

Unless otherwise noted, all Scripture quotations are from the Holy Bible, New International Version of the Bible. Copyright © 1973, 1978, 1984, International Bible Society. Used by permission.

Scripture quotations marked AMP are from the Amplified Bible. Old Testament copyright © 1965, 1987 by the Zondervan Corporation. The Amplified New Testament copyright © 1954, 1958, 1987 by the Lockman Foundation. Used by permission.

Scripture quotations marked HCSB are from the Holman Christian Standard Bible ® Copyright © 2003, 2002, 2000, 1999 by Holman Bible Publishers. Used by permission. All rights reserved.

Scripture quotations marked NKJV are from the New King James Version of the Bible. Copyright © 1979, 1980, 1982 by Thomas Nelson, Inc., publishers. Used by permission.

Design Director: Bill Johnson
Cover design by Terry Clifton

Library of Congress Cataloging-in-Publication Data: 2013941262
International Standard Book Number: 978-1-62136-396-5
E-book International Standard Book Number: 978-1-62136-397-2

First edition

13 14 15 16 17 — 9 8 7 6 5 4 3 2 1

Printed in Canada

DEDICATION

Christ for the World, Inc. (CFTW, Inc.) was founded by the late Dr. and Mrs. E. J. Daniels (what a privilege to have known them both) as a nonprofit mission organization in 1948. Through the years the ministry has been dedicated to conducting missions in single churches or in trans-denominational settings with many churches and large attendance in venues such as stadiums, arenas, and their large three thousand-seat canvas cathedral.

Reverend John Bos joined the organization as associate director in 1972, and served in that capacity until the death of Dr. Daniels in 1987, at which time John became acting director, with Mrs. Daniels serving as general director.

The Reverend Dr. Bos received a Doctorate of Divinity well over a decade ago and a Doctorate of Evangelism from Immanuel Baptist Theological Seminary in Atlanta in April, 2006.

At the death of Mrs. Daniels, Dr. Bos became executive director in September 2000. The ministry continues to organize and direct citywide and area-wide missions and festivals, from start to finish. Pastors and lay leaders are used to organize committees that function in the meetings. All publicity is prepared by CFTW, Inc., and all finances are assumed up front until, and if, expenses are recovered from the budgets. The organization has the lowest festival budgets available and prefers working in county-seat-type towns.

Christ for the World, Inc. also sponsors building projects in developing countries. Churches, schools, orphanages, and Bible institutes are presently complete or in various stages of construction. The locals provide the land in most instances, and CFTW, Inc. supplies the funds. Most building is done by local church members or religious leaders. Construction projects are complete or in progress in India, Kenya, Philippines, Romania, and Ukraine. The goal of the organization is to do its part in fulfilling the Great Commission of Christ (Matt. 28:18–20): "Go into all the world and preach the gospel to every creature." Once each month, Dr. Bos is in a different country performing concerts and speaking in churches and schools.

A Netherlands native, John married his wonderful, godly wife, Shirley. God led them to move to Orlando in 1965, and they became active members of our church. During the next few years, John was gone much of the time in music ministry with Dr. Daniels as well as other evangelists, including some of the Billy Graham Associates. John and Shirley have raised beautiful kids and grandkids. Before I joined the pastoral staff full time, I taught life groups (Sunday school for many of you) for a couple of decades and so enjoyed a few years of teaching John and Shirley's handsome son, Dr. Jeff Bos, and his beautiful wife, Stacey.

For many years, Shirley has faithfully served in various ministries of our church (senior adults, Sunday school, life groups, etc.), and she is currently administrative assistant to our Legacy ministry. Periodically, she travels with John on mission trips, and she is faithful in the CFTW, Inc. Publication, *Family Magazine*. After years of reading their publication, I continue to be amazed at the stories and photos of the enormous crowds who gather to hear John play the piano and organ and then preach the gospel to many who have never heard of Jesus. Only once we get to heaven will we realize how many people have been impacted and souls saved through the ministry of John and Shirley Bos.

Their international ministry is based right here in Orlando and rivals closely behind the number of souls touched by other well-known ministries based here, such as Campus Crusade for Christ, Wycliffe Bible Translators, and Jay Strack Ministries/Student Leadership University. My conservative estimate is between 3.5 and 4 million persons have been blessed by this ministry. John and Shirley asked that I not draw attention to them. The only place I can find in Scripture where Jesus describes His attributes is found in Matthew 11:29: "I am gentle and humble in heart" (HCSB); John and Shirley Bos are just like Jesus and they both offer many touches of Jesus to persons in need of hope.

In 2010, serving as chairman of the Executive Committee of the 16.5 million member Southern Baptist Convention (SBC, based in Nashville), I was asked to travel to Alpharetta, Georgia, location of the North American Mission Board (NAMB), which is an entity of the SBC. NAMB had created the Evangelists Hall of Faith, and I was privileged to participate in the ribbon cutting. The hall recognized outstanding evangelists who were serving under the Conference of Southern Baptist Evangelists (COSBE). I was amazed at the large number of evangelists whom I knew personally: Roy Fish, Cliff Barrows, Sam Cathey, E. J. Daniels, Ron Dunn, Freddie Gage, Billy Graham, Junior Hill, Bailey Smith, T. W. Wilson, and Jay Strack, just to mention a few (Dr. Strack was a member of my ordination council when I was ordained as a pastor). There are a number of equally prominent evangelists I did not mention, but I want you to know the caliber of godly preachers recognized.

It was such a joy to hear Dr. John Bos' name called at the 2012 SBC in New Orleans when the year's inductees were announced. I know John was humbled to follow in the steps of great men like Dr. E. J. Daniels and Dr. Billy Graham, and I am thankful to Dr. David Uth, our senior pastor at First Orlando, for honoring John and Shirley in our Sunday services on July 22, 2012.

Because of the quiet magnitude of the ministries of Dr. John and Shirley Bos, it is my honor to dedicate this book in their honor and in appreciation of Christ for the World, Inc., to the glory of our Lord and Savior Jesus Christ.

"Dr. John and Shirley Bos"

TABLE OF CONTENTS

FOREWORD

By Governor Jeb Bush

IN THE MID-1960s when Walt Disney Productions purchased more than 27,000 acres of land in Central Florida, no one could have estimated, with any degree of accuracy, the impact this development would have on a community unprepared to meet the need. Even the most visionary governmental leaders lacked enough funding in their budgets to provide infrastructure needs for expanding the highway network, sewer capacity for phenomenal growth, expansion of a once-military base converted airport, just to mention a few. Walt Disney World was brilliant in convincing the Florida Legislature and Florida Governor Claude Kirk to make its development practically autonomous with the approval of the Reedy Creek Improvement District. This allowed Disney engineers and planners to use their own magical imaginations in creating a dynamic tourist destination.

For the next quarter of a century, Orange County and Orlando, Disney's neighbors to the northeast, fought to catch up with the growth curve. *Morphing Orlando...into a World-Class City* provides an inside look into the challenges presented by unfunded mandates. I met the author in the mid-1980s when I served as Florida's Secretary of Commerce. Since then, particularly during my two terms as Florida's Governor, I have worked with Randall on projects and events. I know him to be a quiet, behind the scenes leader who has diligently served on staff, boards and commissions for four Orlando mayors and three Orange County mayors. This book offers insider insights into the mechanics involved from groundbreakings to ribbon cuttings.

I support public/private partnerships. One such partnership I was able to support as governor improved traffic safety on I-4's westbound exit at John Young Parkway. Extreme congestion at the main interstate exit serving Central Florida's largest church had caused many serious rear-end crashes. After Randall retired from the City of Orlando and joined the pastoral staff of First Baptist Orlando, he served as one of the point persons for Senior Pastor Jim Henry to work with the Florida Department of Transportation. The church graciously allowed the FDOT to eventually build a flyover ramp atop church property allowing the project to meet budget. In March of 2004, I was honored to join Astronaut John Young, Dr. Henry, and others to break ground on a win-win project for the people of Metro Orlando.

I hope this book will create a greater appreciation for the many men and women government employees, national, state, and local, and the contributions of the vast number of volunteers who help make our communities better places to live, work, and raise families.

—JEB BUSH

Governor Jeb Bush

This miniature flag of the City of Orlando was taken into outer space on the Spacelab I mission by astronaut John Young during the flight of the Space Shuttle "Columbia" November 28, - December 8, 1983.

Spacelab 1 Orlando Flag

Governor Bush, John and Suzy Young

INTRODUCTION

*In the beginning was the Word, and the Word
was with God, and the Word was God.*

–JOHN 1:1

I WAS PRIVILEGED TO serve thirty-one years in government (not including my time in the United States Air Force)—six years as a Rocky Mount, North Carolina police officer, twenty-four and one half years with the City of Orlando, and six months in the Orange County mayor's office. Then, in 1997, God relieved me from government and blessed me as an associate pastor/foundation president of the oldest and largest church in our metro area, First Baptist Church of Orlando (FBC/O).

In this book, it is my hope to share with you some of the inner/behind the scenes workings, most of which I was personally involved with, that helped transform a small, quiet Florida town into one of the most desired tourist destinations in the world. Do you remember when the Florida Department of Motor Vehicles issued automobile license tags beginning with the number ranking of the size of the area where the tags were issued? Before 1978, the population of the county determined the first number on every tag: Miami/Dade was 1, Jacksonville/Duval was 2, Tampa/Hillsborough was 3, Orlando/Orange was 7, and so forth. While working as an Orlando police officer in the early and mid-1970s, this helped me know where the tag was purchased and probably where the owner lived. Today, if the DMV still used this system, Orlando and Orange County tags would all begin with 5, even though in our latest census, Orlando/Orange added more population than every other county except Dade.

It was the year 1977, and I was serving in the Orlando Police Department's (OPD) Community Relations section and assigned as the uniformed sergeant-at-arms for the Monday afternoon City Council meetings. After attending for about one year these rather boring meetings (except for the parts into which Mayor Langford infused frequent humor), the mayor signaled he wanted to speak with me after the meeting. He called me by my first name, Randall—I did not have a clue he knew my first name, as my uniform name badge had only my last name, "JAMES." The mayor asked me how I would like to come to work in his office as administrative aide. Instantly I said, "Yes, sir!" During the next three years of his administration, Langford entrusted me with being his cable TV officer (during a volatile period when cable was slowly coming online accompanied by thousands of citizen complaint calls of busy signals when trying to reach the Orange/Seminole Cablevision office), liaison to Orlando Utilities and the Greater Orlando Aviation Authority, and close confidante.

In November of 1980, Willard Drawn Frederick (even though he went by Bill, most constituents thought his first name was William) defeated Orlando City Commissioner Shelton Adams. I knew Mr. Frederick was a well-known, successful attorney but I did not have a personal relationship with him. In the policies and procedures of the Orlando City Code, there is a provision enacted at the change of mayors requiring the written resignation of the previous administration's mayoral staff. As required by city policy, I submitted my resignation letter (I knew I was covered by civil service and could go back to OPD). My letter was the only one from Langford's staff the new mayor rejected. Thank You, Jesus, for using folks like Jerry Chicone, Bob Snow, and Pete Barr to suggest Frederick keep me on his new team.

Starting with this transition, I began to realize it was divine providence that allowed me to serve as chief of staff at the end of the Langford era, and to serve Mayor Bill Frederick for twelve years (more than half as his chief of staff), and five years as Mayor Hood's chief of staff, until I was called into full time ministry at FBC/O. It is for this reason I thought it might be a simple "thank You, Lord" to begin each chapter with a verse from His Word. At my retirement, the City Council voted me Orlando Chief of Staff Emeritus. This was one of the most humbling awards of my entire career.

Orlando has been blessed with great leadership in the city and the county, and I would not want a single reader to think I am being boastful of anything I did during this period of phenomenal growth. I believe Metro Orlando is the finest community in the nation to live, work, and raise a family. It is my desire to share some insights, events, and tactics we employed in the different administrations to bring us where we are today. Many of them are not commonly known to even the most avid government observer (or newspaper reporter). Some are scary, nerve-wracking, bold, and even downright hilarious. I pray this book will further educate and bless you.

As I gathered my thoughts for each chapter, it made me more cognizant of God's hand on every project which improved the quality of life for Orlandoans. In John 15:5, Jesus is quoted as saying, "...apart from Me you can do nothing." This book covers more than a quarter of a century looking at my life in the public sector and I feel it is appropriate to share a few closing chapters that talk about the spiritual side of my fifteen-year employment as a pastor.

My humble thanks go to one of Florida's finest governors, the Honorable Jeb Bush, my employers, my editorial advisor, Pat Birkhead, my wife, Irma, and our daughter, Lori Shipley, for their wisdom, input, and prayers.

Mayors Frederick, Hood, Dyer, Langford, and Crotty

Jerry Lee Lewis Security

Chapter 1

A NORMANDY MIRACLE

He preserves the lives of His saints; He delivers
them out of the hand of the wicked.

—Psalm 97:10b, amp

June 6, 1944: Operation Overlord

A YOUNG US Army captain, along with his one hundred men from 29th Infantry Division (nicknamed "Blue and Gray"), 116th Infantry Regiment, was transferred by boat to the English Channel off the Normandy coast of France. He and his unit thought they were landing after Allied aircraft had bombed the beach. Unfortunately for them, the attack had not happened. As he and his men jumped from the boat into the water, they may have fortified themselves with their division's motto: "29, let's go!"

The soldiers of the 116th Infantry hit the beach at 06:30, coming under heavy fire from German fortifications. If you have seen the movie *Saving Private Ryan*, you know the brutality of those next hours. By the end of D-Day, 2,400 men from two divisions had become casualties on Omaha Beach. Added to casualties from other beaches and airdrops, the total casualties for Operation Overlord were 6,500 Americans and 3,000 British and Canadians.

The young army captain and his one hundred men lay on the beach. Several hours later a group of US Army nurses walked among the hundreds of bodies, checking for any signs of life. One young lieutenant nurse felt a pulse on only one of the one hundred men:

the army captain. She had him transported to a remote MASH tent barracks in rural France where the nurses and doctors treated US and Russian soldiers.

As Paul Harvey used to say, now here's the rest of the story.

John James grew up in Marmaduke, North Carolina. He began his military service in ROTC and eventually was made an army captain over one hundred men.

Evelyn Wilson, from Fordsville, Kentucky, received her RN at Baptist Hospital, Memphis, Tennessee. She was a member of Bellevue Baptist Church in Cardova, Tennessee. Dr. R.G. Lee was her pastor, and her favorite sermon by Pastor Lee was "Payday Someday." Evelyn joined the army and became a lieutenant. In June 1944, she and her company of army nurses were sent to Paris.

Lieutenant Evelyn Wilson helped stabilize and treat Captain John James, and as he convalesced, they stayed in touch and their feelings for each other blossomed. When his health improved, James was dispatched back to duty in Germany.

As the war ended, Capt. James was reunited with Lt. Wilson in Paris and before being shipped back to the States, they were married by an army chaplain at a beautiful setting on the French Riviera in the presence of a number of their army "buddies."

The US Army awarded Capt. James the Purple Heart, the Award of Valor, the Bronze Star, and numerous other recognitions. His brother, Private First Class Lester James (for whom I was named), was also in the US Army Infantry (Company B) and was killed in action in France on Daddy's birthday, July 17, 1944—he was twenty-four years old. Had it not been for the union of Capt. James and Lt. Wilson on Omaha Beach, I would not have been able to call myself *A Normandy Miracle.*

Lieutenant Evelyn James

Captain John James

Capt. John and Lt. Evelyn James

Chapter 2

ORLANDO'S FINEST

Everyone must submit himself to the governing authorities, for there is no authority except that which God has established. The authorities that exist have been established by God.

–ROMANS 13:1

I SERVED SIX YEARS as an officer on the Rocky Mount, North Carolina Police Department before joining the Orlando Police Department in the spring of 1974. I was disappointed that the State of Florida Criminal Justice Standards and Training Commission would not grant reciprocity for my law enforcement training in North Carolina and required me to be certified by the State of Florida.

When I graduated from the OPD police academy, I stood in amazement at the degree of highly specialized training required. After the police academy training was complete, OPD required several more weeks of "OPD Orientation" to make sure each new officer was thoroughly familiar with their policies and procedures manual. In North Carolina, I was an expert state's witness on the detection of speed—to qualify for this status using the Time/Distance/Speed computer used by Florida Highway Patrol aircraft today, an officer had to detect the speed of one hundred moving vehicles without missing more than two clocked speeds by two miles per hour or more. At OPD, I was assigned as a Breathalyzer operator and administered hundreds of breath tests as an accident investigator. According to numerous national criminal justice publications, OPD is a national model agency, and I am proud to have served with these very professional women and men officers. I made friendships lasting a lifetime.

I was assigned to patrol for two years before being transferred to the Community Relations Section, where I worked one year. I had a passion to investigate motor vehicle wrecks. Even though I was often assigned to the Accident Investigation car, I never referred to these vehicular collisions as "accidents"—in my opinion, someone was always at fault (and usually got a traffic citation). I never recall a tree or fire hydrant jumping in the street in front of a moving vehicle!

You can ask almost any police officer about some of their memorable experiences, and he or she can share some unusual and often hilarious stories. Officers love telling their "war stories." I recall one hot summer midnight shift chasing a car south on Orange Avenue past Orlando City Hall—it was around 3:30 a.m. and there was no traffic. I was clocking the fleeing vehicle at about sixty miles per hour. When the driver tried to make the hard, left curve just past the Orlando Utilities building, his car sailed airborne into Lake Lucerne. As I stopped my patrol car, I watched the driver crawl out his window as the car began to sink. He treaded water for a few minutes ignoring my command to swim to where I stood on the bank. Finally, I yelled out to him, "You are one brave guy in the water with all those alligators! Look! There is a big one swimming right toward you!" I used my bright flashlight to dance on the water beside him and he began swimming like crazy straight to me. By the time he hit shore, he was too tired to resist arrest.

Because of my previous police experience, OPD Chief James Goode personally interviewed me on a Monday morning (at the request of a mutual friend) and asked me if I could come to work at 7:00 a.m. the next day. I assure you this type of OPD employment probably has never occurred since—it was truly a "God thing." Because the next police academy was a month away and since I had experienced officer stress for six years, I was assigned to "west side radio" in the communications section. Radio operators may not experience the danger of physical attacks from suspects, but I assure you, they share the same degree of stress as the officer who is yelling his location while running and trying to give an accurate description of the suspect over his radio. It takes a well-trained ear to correctly relay "panic sounding" directions to responding officers en route to assist.

My first day on west side radio (the busiest of all the communication channels because it covers the highest crime area), I made a friend for life. Motor Officer Thomas D. Hurlburt (Tommy to his close friends) was working the northeast sector of the city when I dispatched him to a call on Bobolink Lane in Audubon Park. When he cleared the call, he drove to the nearest fire phone and asked that he be connected to west side radio. For you young readers who aren't familiar with a "fire phone," there used to be numerous red boxes on telephone poles strategically placed around the city. Inside the box was a phone with no out dial capacity. When the receiver is lifted, the call is automatically connected to an Orlando Fire Department dispatcher who would dial any local number for the officer. Because of the prominence of cell phones, these fire phones are no longer needed or in existence.

I was born and lived in North Carolina for over twenty years, and when I began work at OPD, I had a fairly strong Southern accent. I feel I have lost most of it over the years, but certainly not that first week working in OPD communications. Officer Hurlburt's first words to me from the fire phone were, "Hey, Hoss—where're you from?" After telling him, he said, "You are the first person on radio I can understand every word!" He, too, had a very Southern accent, and to this day when we talk, we both automatically revert to our own dialect! Over the years, Tommy and Carolyn have become precious friends to Irma and me, and we have enjoyed traveling and dining together. However, one of our many joys is telling war stories about Mayors Langford, Frederick, and Hood—stories we can't always tell in public.

One of my patrol duties on day shift led me to another lifelong friendship. At the beginning of my OPD career there were only six black OPD officers and an even smaller number of women officers. Whenever it rained, I was assigned to go to Lake Eola Park and pick up Officer Belvin Perry, Sr. to ride the rest of the shift with me or until it quit raining. After joining the Florida Bar, Belvin Jr. became a friend because of my love for his Dad and later, Belvin Jr. became a judge. He served as an assistant state attorney and later became Chief Judge of the Ninth Judicial Circuit. Judge Perry may be most remembered for the awesome way he conducted the Casey Anthony murder trial. I began to love Belvin like a blood brother and would do anything I could to help him in his professional and/or private life. I recall Belvin and I serving on a committee to bring well-known youth evangelist Josh McDowell to a crusade in the UCF gym, and Belvin's son responding to Josh's invitation.

I would like to mention two other black officers with whom I was privileged to serve. At one point, Lieutenant R.A. Jones (we called him Ra Ra) was my watch commander, and God gave me instant favor with him. The other officer with whom I loved working cases was Officer Otha Lee Kelly. In a time not far removed from segregation, these officers were shining examples of promoting unity among races. I never thought of them as black officers; they were brothers to me whom I loved having as back-up, and I was honored to be called to back them up.

I wish time and space allowed me to share with you a few more "war stories." But in closing I must mention the most awkward predicament I ever faced as an officer.

I got a call to a "car versus tree." Nothing unusual about that except that upon my arrival, I found the driver, a beautiful young woman in her twenties, hiding behind the bushes, totally nude. She had driven her car into a large oak tree because she was so under the influence of drugs (no detection of any alcohol odor). Remember the old *Candid Camera* spin-off television program, *What Do You Say to A Naked Lady?* That was my question. With all the diplomacy and grace I could muster, I asked, "Are you hurt?" She responded, "No—I just want to kiss you!" Since a crowd had assembled and no backup officer was readily en route, I gently yet professionally asked her to go to my car so we could talk. As she began walking to me, under my breath I whispered, "Help me, Jesus!"

When she was about three feet away, she dived into my arms, locked both legs around my waist (like my grandkids used to do), and tried to put a lip lock on me. I yelled, "Stop. I want to get a blanket out of my trunk and wrap it around you." She was not interested, and when she realized I was not going to accommodate her amorous offer, she became combative. Keep in mind that a lot of spectators were watching my hands as much as her well-endowed body. I told her she was under arrest and she immediately kicked me in my private area so hard I wanted to throw up. My adrenaline kicked into high gear and we both went to the ground as I reached for my handcuffs. At this point, I never gave another thought to where my hands may have brushed her body. When I did get her in cuffs, I threw her over my shoulder and was putting her in the back of my car when another police unit arrived to assist. The folks in that trailer park were treated with quite a show—one that I will never forget!

Chief Paul Rooney

Marshal Hurlburt and Chase Shipley

The first black Orlando police officers in 1957 (from left): Richard Arthur Jones, John W. Jordan, Gainous Wright, Mayo Howard, Belvin Perry Sr. and Otha Lee Kelly.

OPD Officers

OPD Officer James

Lori Ann James

Chapter 3

HIZZONER THE MAYOR

Unless the LORD watches over the city, the
watchmen stand guard in vain.
−PSALM 127:1B

O F THE FOUR Orlando mayors I served, I believe Mayor Carl T. Langford, "Call me by my first name, 'Mayor,'" is the most intriguing, fascinating elected CEO I have ever known. In fact, this "character" is mentioned quite a few times in this book.

In 1971, I was assigned as an Orlando Police Community Relations Officer, often serving every Monday as sergeant-at-arms at City Council meetings. After about one year of this duty, Mayor Langford walked over to me after the adjournment and called me by my first name, Randall. I had no idea he knew my name as our OPD uniforms displayed only the officer's last name on the shirt pocket nameplate. "How would you like to come to work in my office as an administrative aide?" he asked. Before I could take another breath, I calmly replied, "Yes, sir, I would be honored!"

I don't think I have ever been so stunned, yet elated, since Irma said, "Yes, I would love to marry you!" I had been a sworn officer for the Rocky Mount, North Carolina Police Department for six years prior to relocating to Orlando, but I had been on OPD for only three years. I was sworn in by the Mayor Pro Tem, Commissioner Arthur "Pappy" Kennedy, the city of Orlando's first African American Commissioner.

After a half day of orientation by two secretarial assistants and staff director Tom Kohler, I was left finding out most everything else by trial and error and asking a lot of questions. In those days, the mayor's office housed the phone lines of the city commissioners as well as four push-button lines for the mayor. In essence, the mayor's staff also served as the commissioners' staff. There were four districts represented by Commissioners Don Crenshaw, George Stuart, Bob Keith, and Arthur Kennedy. Thinking back about our four-member staff answering, referring, investigating, etc., every citizen's complaint to the mayor and four commissioners makes me wonder how in the world we managed the office so efficiently (only by the grace of God)! During Mayor Bill Frederick's administration the city was enlarged by annexation as well as going from four to six districts. The expansion necessitated that each commissioner be allowed to hire an aide for each district, and a city commission staff director was hired.

Back to CTL (this was the staff code for Mayor Carl Thomas Langford). If you found favor with him—and you had to have favor to remain on the team—he was the epitome of respectfulness and thoughtfulness. Each December, he would pass out to the four of us a list of approximately twenty-five household items (toothpaste, deodorant, shampoo, soap, washing powder, cereal, hair spray, dishwasher liquid, and your favorite soda—and this is less than half the list) with a hyphen and a blank beside each item. His instructions to me were to get each blank filled with a brand name of each item, and then drive him to a large grocery warehouse down on Kaley Street, where he and I would fill the orders. It truly made for a most practical Christmas gift, and he was such a generous boss! Now, as Paul Harvey would say (God rest both of their souls), I feel like I can tell you "the rest of the story."

The mayor would slip in my office right after he passed out the "grocery lists" for each of us, and hand me several sales paper inserts from the Thanksgiving edition of the local paper; e.g. Radio Shack, Sears, Montgomery Ward. On each page, he would have circled two or three items ranging from a police scanner or television set to a refrigerator, and he would say, "Just in case the appointed officials might want to pitch in for a few Christmas gifts for the mayor." Well, thank the Lord, we had enough appointed officials that each year we were able to "fill his Christmas stocking" with every item on the lists without putting too much of a dent in our wallets.

United States Marshal Tom Hurlburt (who also worked for CTL prior to myself) and Orlando City Clerk Emeritus Grace Ann Chewning may have more Mayor Langford stories than I, but not many! In preparing to write this chapter—which is also the title of Mayor Langford's book—I was flooded with so many memories I think would be of interest to our citizens that someday I may have to write a book just about him.

I believe every aspiring "wanna-be" politician should read *Hizzoner the Mayor*. It has some of the finest campaign strategies I know. I do cherish the most gracious, humbling note he penned in the front cover of my copy, dated July 23, 1978—which just happened to be his sixtieth birthday. His note most certainly restrains me from telling a few of the hilarious stories of which my wife would not approve!

A sample of his sage counsel: "One important thing to keep in mind is that, if you are a candidate, you should adopt a mental attitude of running on your own merit and not the other man's demerits...try not to admit that there's anybody else in the campaign, but if you're forced to acknowledge him, you must refer to him as 'the other candidate.' Whatever you do, don't refer to him by his proper name. Let him spend money if he wants to advertise his name but don't help him."[1]

Born in Orlando, the mayor was educated in Orlando schools and graduated with honors from the University of Florida, where he was Chancellor of the Honor Court. He served in the United States Army from 1941–1946 and was granted an honorable discharge as a major.

In 1967, when he was first elected as mayor of Orlando, he removed the front door of his office confirming his open-door policy. Actually, he used a smaller side room (not visible from the glass wall

---

1 Carl Langford, *Hizzoner the Mayor* (Orlando, FL: Chateau Publishing Inc., 1976), 22–23.

dividing his suite from the hall) to concentrate on quiet work—on the door was a sign, "Bureau of Public Apathy."

On afternoons when he met with constituents, vendors, and community leaders, he would greet them beside his large desk and invite them to have a seat in one of the comfortable chairs in front of his desk. He had the head of a parking meter on top of his desk, and would insert a nickel in the meter at the beginning of each meeting. The red "expired" slot would fall and the meter would read "15 minutes," as the working meter began ticking down. At the onset, the mayor would tell each appointment they had fifteen minutes and if that was not enough time they would have to set another appointment at a future date. No matter how important a person he met, I never recall a time when he did not stand when the meter expired, thank them for their input, and bid them farewell.

Mayor Langford had a particular affinity for retired military officers and for active and retired police officers. I think this was because he had been successful in the United States Army, graduated from the Orlando Police Academy, and was a sworn police officer authorized to carry a firearm. Many of his major appointed city department heads were retired military personnel and they served him well. He did more to improve resources and pay for Orlando police than any mayor in modern times. His son, Tommy, worked his way up from officer and retired as a lieutenant (with no influence from Dad, but on the merits of his test scores).

As a commissioner on the Orlando Utilities Commission (OUC)—the utilities are owned by the City of Orlando, as is the Orlando International Airport—Mayor Langford helped direct annually shared OUC profits to the city to build a new police headquarters. The building was initially named the Municipal Justice Building but today is named Orlando Police Headquarters.

After Mayor Langford decided not to run for reelection in 1980, he and his wife, Marietta, moved to their home on the side of the mountain behind Stuckey's in Maggie Valley, North Carolina. The view from his front porch was one of the most beautiful I have ever seen. They enjoyed retirement there until Marietta's health deteriorated and they moved back to Orlando.

When Marietta passed away several years ago, Mayor Langford called and asked me to preach her funeral. In the years after her death, he began to call me at least once a month and asked me many spiritual questions. I could tell he was under conviction—the Bible says in Romans 3:23–24, "for all have sinned and fall short of the glory of God, and all are justified freely by his grace through the redemption that came by Christ Jesus." He shared with me on a number of occasions that he had asked Jesus to forgive him of his sins.

Finally, on July 1, 2011, I was convicted by the Holy Spirit to go to Mayor Langford's daughter's home where he lived and speak with him face-to-face about his faith. I asked my closest friend and his closest friend, US Marshal Tom Hurlburt, who is a committed believer, to go with me so Mayor Langford would feel more comfortable. That day, the marshal and I helped him understand clearly the simplicity of accepting the free gift of salvation; two weeks later, I preached Mayor Langford's Celebration of Life service. The graveside service followed at Greenwood Cemetery—a place the mayor always referred to as the "dead center of town"—and the US Army's horse drawn caisson carrying his flag-draped casket ran chills down my spine. I look forward to the day I will be with Mayor and Marietta Langford again.

Mayor Langford at Desk

Mayor Frederick and Mayor Langford

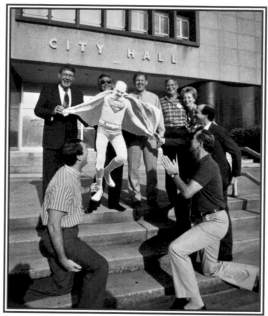

Mayor Langford's Team: (left to right) Tom Kohler, John Wyckoff, Yogi Moore, Tom Hurlburt, Randall James, Grace Chewning, Paul Rosenthal, and Egerton Van den Berg

Mayor Langford with TriCounty League Tombstone

Mayor Langford and President Gerald Ford

Mayor Langford Playing Taps at End of Last Term

Chapter 4

BASEBALL STARS
IN ORLANDO

Delight yourself in the LORD *and he will*
give you the desires of your heart.

—PSALM 37:4

S A VERY young boy growing up in Rocky Mount, North
Carolina, some of my fondest memories were of playing
baseball on small fry, little league, and pony league teams. I
proudly wore number seven in honor of my Major League Baseball
(MLB) hero, Mickey Mantle, one of the greatest players ever to wear
the Yankee pinstripes!

I lived four blocks from Municipal Stadium, home of the Rocky
Mount Leafs, farm club of the Cincinnati Reds. My daddy's business took care of the team bus as hardly any of the players had cars.
They rented near the stadium and would walk the ten or twelve
blocks to my daddy's business and hang out when they had free time.
The two players who "took a liking to me" were Tony Perez and
Cesar Tovar, third and second basemen, respectively. Neither future
superstar spoke good English, and Tony would often help me understand Cesar's words. I loved them, and they loved me so much they
both went to the manager seeking permission for me to accompany
them on the team bus—what a thrill!

By the way, Tony Perez went on to become a member of the MLB
Hall of Fame in 2000, and Cesar still holds a number of records
(he was the second player in history to play all nine positions in

one game). After Cesar's MLB career, he went back to play in his native Venezuela, where he (before he died of cancer) was inducted into the Venezuelan Baseball Hall of Fame. Perez, a key member of Cincinnati's "Big Red Machine," went on to become manager of the Cincinnati Reds and the Florida Marlins. I will remember these two stars until I die.

After moving to Orlando in 1974, I became an Orlando Police Department officer, and today hold the rank of Lieutenant Retired. I went to work on Mayor Langford's staff in February of 1977. He was the most eccentric man for whom I ever worked, yet he was very intelligent and had an amazing memory. I went to an Orlando Jaycees meeting with him one night. When he was introduced to speak, he named every man in the room but two by their first and last names, and he recalled the first names of the other two! I will have more to say about him later, but Mayor Langford knew how much I loved baseball, and often during the Minnesota Twins Spring Training games at Tinker Field (next to the Tangerine Bowl, then—now the Citrus Bowl), he would have me take one of his most ardent supporters to many afternoon games—what a tough job!

On December 5, 1978, I drove the mayor to the Sheraton Twin Towers to welcome the National Association of Professional Baseball Leagues—I had cold chills when I walked in the room and recognized so many baseball stars. I asked the mayor if he would be offended if I took our large invitation card and got a few autographs. He said, "Have at, RJ!" As I sit here at my computer, I am reading you some of the names of autographs in one of my scrapbooks. The first person to sign my card was the "Yankee Clipper, Joltin' Joe" DiMaggio, thirteen-time All Star Hall of Famer, and Stan "The Man" Musial, followed by Pete Rose, Johnny Bench, George Steinbrenner, Calvin Griffith, Don Drysdale, Gene Mauch, Chub Feeney, Bob Lemon, Ron Guidry, the "late, great" Ted Williams, Joe Garagiola, Lee MacPhail, Ernie Banks, Joe Cronin, Bowie Kuhn, Bobby Bragan, Warren Giles, and others. One of my most prized autographs was from the special guest, and it reads, "My Best Always, Jesse Owens—'36 Olympics!" The entertainment for the evening was "The Bill Anderson Show" featuring Bill Anderson and Roy Acuff.

This is a night I will forever cherish from my younger years. In my humble opinion, The City Beautiful will never again host such a large number of stars in one room (unless you combine the total number of National Basketball Association's All Stars playing in the Orlando Arena in 1992 and the Amway Center in 2012).

Front of Autograph Card

Chapter 5

PRO FOOTBALL IN ORLANDO

I press on toward the goal to win the prize.
–Philippians 3:14

I LOVE COMPETITIVE SPORTS and have been blessed to attend three Super Bowls. Super Bowl X was played in Miami's Orange Bowl on January 19, 1976, and one of my close high school buddies was starting guard for the Pittsburgh Steelers—#50, Jim Clack. Jim's mother, Mable Clack, was my Sunday school teacher for many elementary school years.

A few days before the game, Jim called to see if I was coming—if so, he wanted to see me. Irma got us two awesome tickets on the second row right on the fifty yard line. She introduced me to the man who provided our tickets—needless to say, I gained a new, faithful friend, Ray Dorman, who served as Assistant Athletic Director (AD) under Florida Gator AD Coach Ray Graves, who just happened to have played for the Pittsburgh Steelers and is the winningest Gator head coach only behind Steve Spurrier. When I told Jim where we would be sitting, he instructed me to try to get his attention in the pre-game warm-ups (he knew I was a loud whistler). Only God could have helped him hear me in that pack of humanity, and he ran over to the low wall and gave us both a hug. He told me he would be back during the game and for us to keep our eye on him.

When the first quarter ended, he came running over to where we were seated and asked Irma if it was OK for me to go with him. I don't remember her answer, but I hopped on that field in a flash and Jim led me to the Steelers' bench. Clack was 6'5", 238 pounds, but with cleats and helmets on, they were all giants. I was six feet tall, but the only way I could see over the players was to stand on the bench—what a thrill!

I remained on the bench the remainder of the game and the Steelers beat the Cowboys 21–17 on a "Hail Mary" pass interception in the end zone (from Dallas quarterback, Roger Staubach). After the final whistle, Jim told me to follow him into the clubhouse (today, the winning team stays on the field for trophy presentations). As the champagne corks popped in front of a host of handheld TV cameras, I got to high-five players like Terry Bradshaw, Rocky Bleier, "Mean" Joe Greene, L.C. Greenwood, Lynn Swann, John Stallworth, Franco Harris, and Jack Lambert to name a few!

Oh, how I wish to this day the NFL had a team in Orlando. We had the Continental League here from 1966 to 1969 when our star quarterback, Don Jonas, led the Florida Blazers to back-to-back championships in '67 and '68. In 1970, Jonas went on to play in the Canadian Football League for five seasons. In 1979, he became the first head football coach for the University of Central Florida. Coach Jonas invited Mayor Bill Frederick to do the ceremonial first kickoff in UCF's new football program. I remember we drove over to an empty Citrus Bowl for the mayor to practice kicking the football from a tee—he did really well on game night.

In my humble opinion, the most exciting pro football to be played in Orlando happened when my dear friend Donald Dizney, founder of United Medical Corporation, bought the financially strapped Washington Federals of the United States Football League (USFL), changed their name to the Orlando Renegades, and played the 1995 season at the Citrus Bowl. The team drew nearly 25,000 fans per game. Our new head coach was Lee Corso, former Florida State University head football coach (later he served as head coach at the University of Louisville, Indiana University, and Northern Illinois University). During the '95 season, the USFL sued the NFL in an antitrust lawsuit and USFL team owners met here in Orlando to discuss strategy. Mr. Dizney invited me to an owners' luncheon at a local hotel and placed me right beside Donald Trump, owner of the New Jersey Generals. I was so intimidated that I just kept my mouth shut, except for a few pleasantries. Mr. Trump was very kind and polite to me—and he didn't fire me!

The next pro football venture in Orlando came from the World Football League. The Orlando Thunder played a couple of seasons and in 1992 made it to the World Bowl, where they lost to the Sacramento Surge. The World League of American Football was followed by the XFL featuring the Orlando Rage. Our team had an 8–2 record, the best in the XFL, but the league folded at the end of the season.

In early 1995, I really got excited when the office of Oakland Raiders owner, Al Davis, called Mayor Glenda Hood and asked for a private, confidential appointment with Mr. Davis in her office—we were all sworn to secrecy, and the mayor asked that I work out details to avoid media exposure. We had not been in our new city hall long, and this would be my first opportunity to use the tunnel from the back of city hall under Boone Street and up to our loading docks.

I met Al Davis around 6:00 p.m. at the city hall loading dock, and walked him through the tunnel and up to our third floor suite of mayoral offices. I had staff prepare a nice, small dinner table up on the ninth floor and had our Centroplex staff turn on the Citrus Bowl lights so we could have a nice view during our intimate dinner—just the three of us. After dinner I drove Mayor Hood and Mr. Davis to the Citrus Bowl, where our Centroplex director, Bill Becker, was waiting to take us on a full tour of the stadium.

Like him or not (and Al Davis had a very public history of not caring at times), I found the man to be very kind, polite, and charming—and it didn't hurt that Mayor Hood seemed to have, unknowingly to them both, smitten him somewhat. I know because it did not take me long to see how much she was charming him. A number of times as we walked, he would lean over to me (away from her hearing) and ask me personal questions about her reputation as a businesswoman and her popularity with her constituency. Once he told me, "she sure is cute for a mayor of a city like Orlando." He was fascinated to say the least and made me think we had an outside chance of getting the Raiders here.

Now I was born at night, but not last night! I knew from the media that Mr. Davis was exploring moving the Raiders back and forth from Oakland to Los Angeles (the Raiders played in Oakland from 1982–1994) and was not shy about wanting a new stadium. Was he leveraging a possible move to Orlando? Well, maybe before he arrived, but I am convinced that after he toured the facility he saw great possibilities with a remodeled Citrus Bowl. The number one attraction (and he must have mentioned it a half dozen times as he spoke to a couple of his advisors who spent a full week inspecting and measuring the Citrus Bowl) was the proximity of the fan base to the actual playing field. He liked the intimacy it created and thought he could sell out each game. Discussions with his staff and ours continued for weeks after Mr. Davis returned to California. Move or no move, I was ecstatic with the time I got to spend with this pro football legend.

Al Davis hired the National Football League's (NFL) first black head coach, Art Shell, in 1988; he hired the first Latino head coach, Tom Flores, and the first woman NFL CEO, Amy Trask. Mr. Davis died recently at the age of eighty-two.

Since 1991, Arena League Football (AFL) fans have enjoyed watching the Orlando Predators play in the old Orlando Arena and now in our beautiful new Amway Center. I will never forget Perry Moss calling me for an appointment—he needed help with our Centroplex staff regarding negotiations to allow the Predators to play in the Orlando Arena. Perry played for the Green Bay Packers and later became head football coach at Florida State University. In 1991, Perry Moss became the first head football coach for the Orlando Predators. Rules for AFL and the size of the indoor playing field are different from the NFL, but Predator fans electrify the "Jungle!"

In the summer of 2012, the City of Orlando and Orange County reached an agreement on funding much-needed improvements to our aging Citrus Bowl. When these improvements are complete (and if it turns out as nice as the conceptual drawings show), I am going to begin praying the Orlando Sports Commission can convince the Tampa Bay Bucs to move to Orlando. I would highly recommend they contract Don Dizney to use his influence to create the Orlando Buccaneers of the NFL.

Don Dizney and Coach Lee Corso

Randall and Irma at Super Bowl X

Rolling Stones Concert in Citrus Bowl

Al Davis

Chapter 6

FREDERICK FOR SHERIFF

But if you do wrong, be afraid, for he does
not bear the sword for nothing.
—ROMANS 13:4

I N MAY OF 1988, I was hospitalized with colon cancer and was in between a successful cancer removal surgery and the implementation of a temporary colostomy. As I lay watching the noon news, I nearly jerked the IVs out of my arms when I sprang out of my hospital bed to get closer to the television news program's lead story! Let me give a little history for the reason I was so excited.

Mayor Carl Langford, the only Orlando mayor ever to complete the Orlando Police Academy, always had a handgun nearby. But in November of 1978 when San Francisco mayor George Moscone was shot to death, I began to look for ways to tighten our mayor's security.

I carried this same concern when I became Mayor Bill Frederick's chief of staff. Frederick was somewhat of a maverick (I mean that in a respectful way), and he was a licensed gun dealer. He had so many sophisticated weapons in those days that he rivaled the old city hall vault, which housed multiplied dozens of Langford's firearms—they ranged from an inconspicuous .22 caliber ballpoint pen pistol to machine guns. I scheduled a firearms training class for Mayor Bill and, upon completion, I placed a .38 caliber Chief's Special in the glove compartment of the mayor's city-owned Oldsmobile 98. In the mid-1980s, I replaced that weapon with a 9mm Beretta, one of the mayor's favorite weapons of choice.

On that morning in May, the mayor drove to Ronnie's Restaurant to meet a constituent for breakfast. For those of you who don't remember, Ronnie's was a Jewish delicatessen on East Colonial Drive that was owned and operated by Larry Leckart, one of our community's most well-known restaurateurs in those days. It was a very popular meeting place for local celebrities, politicians, and the everyday regular Joe. It was a sad day in 1995 when the thirty-nine-year-old landmark was closed for good.

Now back to the story: When Mayor Frederick paid his tab and headed for the car, he observed a man stabbing his estranged wife with a screwdriver. The mayor yelled at the man to stop, and when he ignored Frederick's warning, the mayor didn't hesitate to run to his glove compartment, grab the Beretta, chase the man, and fire a warning shot into the air. At this point, the guy stopped and Mayor Frederick held his foot on the prone suspect until Orlando police arrived. Officers arrested the man and charged him with attempted murder, aggravated battery, and burglary to an occupied vehicle.

As you can imagine, the community was abuzz about the gun-toting mayor, and it was not long before "FREDERICK FOR SHERIFF" bumper stickers appeared everywhere. I don't think I ever heard a derogatory remark about the mayor's actions—he was a hero to nearly everyone who felt he saved that lady's life. Oh yes, I did hear a little grumbling from one of the Orlando Police Union leaders who did not think it was fair for the mayor to have a 9mm weapon before all of the officers were so equipped (about half already had the Sig Sauer 9mm).

This incident was indicative of Orlando's chief executive officer's willingness to step out and risk doing what he thought was right. I believe history will record Mayor Frederick as one of the more visionary Orlando mayors. He was not afraid to risk criticism for making improvements.

I recall when our Orlando Utilities director advised the mayor that we had a water pipe leaking under the surface of Orange Avenue just north of city hall. The recommendation was to dig up a number of blocks and replace the entire line versus doing a "patch job." When Frederick advised the City Council he was giving the Orlando Utilities Commission (OUC) the go-ahead with the work, the story was in the newspaper the next day. This prompted an outcry from the merchants on both sides of Orange Avenue—many said the city would put them out of business. The mayor tried to allay their concerns by promising to "streetscape" with pavers, plants, and other improvements for all of Orange Avenue that had to be unearthed. None of the business owners were happy, but they struggled through and then praised the mayor for a beautiful end product.

The mayor wanted to do a similar beautification to Lake Eola Park. Community criticism from frequent park users was rampant until the project was complete. Taking all of those many citizen complaints was well worth the numerous compliments generated by the new beauty of our landmark centerpiece.

Other major projects that produced much debate included the building of the new Orlando Arena and the new Orlando City Hall. By this time, Frederick was a master of "doing the right thing" for the good of the citizenry. But perhaps the most important project of the Frederick Administration was the most downplayed, as we tried to avoid a building moratorium. Believe me, there was a significant degree of worry behind closed doors at the prospect of a booming metro being ordered to discontinue issuance of building permits.

The court had issued a consent decree to the City of Orlando to stop discharging the city's effluent into Shingle Creek, which flows into Lake Tohopekaliga (we call it Lake Toho for short). There was concern we were polluting the massive lake, and the judge said, "Stop!" Effluent is liquid that flows out and can be treated to the degree it is safe to drink. But the perception of the majority of Osceola County residents was that Orlando was polluting Toho, and the judge agreed. We considered "deep well injection" as a way to dispose of the effluent—that went over like a lead balloon to those who had wells.

Mayor Frederick had the vision to recruit the smartest environmental engineer in the nation to come to help us solve the problem. Bob Haven was a top government engineer in the Washington DC area, and it was not long before the mayor hired him as our public works director (he later became Orlando's chief administrative officer and eventually executive director of Orlando Utilities). Bob and his team developed the Water Conserv II program to dispense our cleaned-up wastewater discharges for use on citrus groves irrigation in West Orange County. The project won numerous national and international engineering awards.

I am so proud to have been on Mayor Frederick's team that helped morph Orlando ahead of the infrastructure curve not only to avoid building moratoriums but also to lead Orlando toward the status of a world-class city. Mayor Frederick helped cut the ribbon on our amazing international airport and later helped steer the aviation authority to approve tremendous expansions that will continue beyond my lifetime.

And it is not just the infrastructure advancements of the city of Orlando, but Orange County has been blessed with visionary leadership as well, from mayors Linda Chapin, Mel Martinez, Rich Crotty, and Teresa Jacobs. Joint planning and designing by city, county, state, and federal agencies have led us today to the awesome Lake Nona Medical City (which includes the Veteran's Administration Hospital, the University of Central Florida College of Medicine, and the Sanford-Burnham Medical Research Institute). The downtown Dr. Phillips' Performing Art Center and the new Amway Center are amenities that draw Fortune 500 companies to our city. We are blessed with the very clean industries of Campus Crusade for Christ and Wycliffe Bible Translators, both with their international headquarters in Metro Orlando. If the above weren't enough, The City Beautiful is the number one tourist destination in America.

Bumper Stickers

Frederick T-Shirt

Dr. Phillips Performing Arts Center

UCF Med School at Lake Nona Medical City

Veteran's Hospital at Lake Nona Medical City

Nemours Children's Hospital at Lake Nona Medical City

Sanford Burnham Medical Research Institute

Chapter 7

"FLOAT LIKE A BUTTERFLY, STING LIKE A BEE!"

Do not think of yourself more highly than you ought, but rather think of yourself with sober judgment, in accordance with the measure of faith God has given you.

—ROMANS 12:3

I HAVE BEEN PONDERING this book for a number of years—I am sure more than one hundred friends have encouraged me to write it, especially those who have thumbed through my photo albums depicting some of the "cool" opportunities God has given me in my government ministry as well as serving as one of His pastors at First Orlando. Even though the miracles Jesus has performed in my life are the epitome of my blessings, He has allowed me to live life abundantly in the secular world. It is my firm conviction that my heavenly Father has approved of me sharing some of these events with you.

I'm sure when you read the title of this chapter, many of you knew immediately who said the title phrase—Cassius Clay (now known as Muhammad Ali). As a young man who loved all kinds of sports and played a lot of baseball in Small Fry, Little League®, and PONY leagues, I loved boxing. I will never forget when my daddy bought our family our first black-and-white television set in the 1950s. I was never allowed to stay up past 10:00 p.m. except on Friday nights to watch boxing with my daddy, boxing presented by Gillette Cavalcade of Sports. I have never quit being a boxing fan.

As chief of staff to Orlando Mayor Bill Frederick (who liked to travel—a lot), I got to represent him on many of the invitations he declined and sent his regrets for "being out of town." Two of them involved the opportunity on separate occasions to have dinner with two famous boxing champions—Muhammad Ali and Smokin' Joe Frazier. I don't know why God allowed me to have favor with Ali, but he offered to have me send him a photo taken of the two of us so he could personally autograph it in real gold ink—I will treasure it always.

I had the privilege of taking my wife, Irma, to dinner with Joe Frazier (pro record of 32–4–1 with 27 knockouts) to a very nice restaurant in downtown Orlando. Frazier was the World Heavyweight Champion in the late 1950s and early 1960s and defeated Ali once and lost to him only twice. The greatest fight between these two champions was in 1975, often called the "Thrilla in Manila." I remember in the fourteenth round Joe's trainer, Eddie Futch, threw in the towel to stop the fight. It was fairly obvious that Joe quickly developed a crush on my very pretty wife—or so it seemed to me—and he spent most of our time at the dinner table getting to know more about us both.

After dinner, we took him to an Orlando Magic game (it was our inaugural NBA season) and I had reserved the mayor's Skybox for Mr. Frazier and his entourage. I had shared with him that even though I was the mayor's chief of staff, I was also a lieutenant with the Orlando Police Department and would be happy to give his limousine a blue light and siren escort with my unmarked police vehicle to the Orlando Arena. Immediately he responded, "Hey, would you mind if I let Irma ride in the limo and I ride with you in your police car?" It took me less than a second to say, "Deal!"

When we arrived at the Skybox entrance to the arena and he and I stepped out to walk back to his limo, a crowd had already quickly gathered to see the VIP stepping out of the limo. Joe asked Irma, "Ma'am, may I have the honor of escorting you up to the Skybox?" What a memorable evening we had! Thank You, Jesus!

Joe Frazier died in 2011 from liver cancer.

Muhammad Ali

Chapter 8

LAKE EOLA PARK'S ASIAN FLAIR

*Look to the rock from which you were cut and
to the quarry from which you were hewn.*

—ISAIAH 51:1

ONE OF MY responsibilities as chief of staff for Mayor Bill Frederick was to oversee Orlando's Sister City (SC) programs. I wrote one SC program for Mayor Carl Langford between Orlando and Bogotá, Columbia, and several for Mayor Glenda Hood. One may know the names of all of our sister cities by reading the "weather vane" pole located in the International Plaza on the south side of Lake Eola Park (where the farmer's market is held each weekend). There are two significant features on opposite sides of Lake Eola Park that were imported from Asia—one from Tainan, Taiwan, ROC (Republic of China); the other from Guilin, China, PRC (People's Republic of China).

In 1982, Mayor Frederick and his sweet wife, Joanne (I reminded him often that he overachieved in marriage), led a small delegation to Tainan for the formal signing of the agreement. Our mayor took a legal briefcase that he had used as an attorney filled with "I Love Orlando" pins, Disney watches (very popular in China), keys to The City Beautiful, plaques, and other small gifts such as chewing gum, yo-yos, and items that brought joy to the many school kids visited by our delegation.

The mayor of Tainan at the time was Su Nan-cheng, and he

insisted on first sending a gift from the citizens of his city before leading a similar-sized delegation from Tainan to Orlando to sign local agreements here. The only information we were given about the gift was that it was a black rock from the top of one of their mountains and that it was "sculpted by the winds for over 10,000 years." They placed the rock on the proverbial "slow boat from China," and during its journey we received instructions from Mayor Su that they wanted it placed "in your great Walt Disney World."

Several months later in May 1983, I received a call from Immigration Services in Jacksonville requesting that we come and process the gift through immigration—and they suggested I bring a *big* truck. I waited until I arrived at the Port of Jacksonville to see how big a truck we would need to rent. To my utter astonishment, the rock was a twelve-ton, very tall, black marble "monument!" Needless to say, I acquired a lowboy semi tractor trailer to bring home our gift.

When I got the "Mayor's Pet Rock" (so named by our city employees) back to Orlando and unloaded at the city's fleet maintenance yard, I called my friend Dick Nunis, chairman of Walt Disney Attractions, to advise him of Mayor Su's desire to erect the monument on Disney property. I will never forget Dick's response: "Randall, where in the world would we put that rock?" Deep in my heart, I was hoping he would say no because the people of Orlando could not enjoy the gift if it was located ten miles south of our city. Mayor Frederick assigned me to bring him a recommendation of where the black marble should be "planted." Lake Eola Park was the unanimous decision. When you look at the stone (or the photo of the stone), you only see the top one-third of this massive black marble. To insure the stone would never blow over, sway, or tilt, two-thirds of this 24,000 pound "statue" had to be buried under the park's surface. Still, it protrudes more than twenty feet above ground.

Elsewhere I mention my dear friend and attorney Jim Robinson, who was, ironically, the Orange County attorney secretly negotiating with Mr. Walt Disney and his lawyers the legal establishment of the Reedy Creek Improvement District (more familiarly known to the rest of the world as Walt Disney World). On the afternoon of December 4, 1983, Jim called me and said he had just begun sub-scribing to *The New York Times* and got his first daily paper that day. He said, "I could not believe my eyes when I saw your name in a story on the front page of one of our nation's largest newspapers." I confirmed *The New York Times* had called me a few weeks earlier to talk about the "huge" gift our citizens received from Tainan. The *Times* entitled the article, "Wind Sculpture," and quoted me several times.

If a twelve ton gift was not big enough, the PRC would not be outdone by the ROC, and sent an even larger gift to commemo-rate our Sister City program in Guilin, China. Dr. Nelson Ying, president of the China Group, which operates the China Pavilion at EPCOT Center in Walt Disney World, negotiated with Mayor Frederick and myself the establishment of the SC program between the two number-one tourist destinations in America and mainland China.

Mayor Frederick graciously paid my way to go to Guilin with him and our local delegation. A decade later, I was privileged to visit again with Mayor Glenda Hood.

Dr. Ying, born in China, selected Guilin because it was the city in China most resembling Orlando. I can attest Guilin as one of the most beautiful cities in the world, with strange looking moun-tains overlooking the majestic Li River. If you visit the 360 degree movie at EPCOT'S China Pavilion, you will be in awe of another "city beautiful." Guilin is also the number-one tourist destination of the 1.3 billion people living in China today (about 20 percent of the seven billion people on earth) and is located in the south of China in a mild climate similar to Orlando's. Tourism is their number one industry—a truly natural match with Orlando.

Photographs cannot do justice to the beauty of the mountains of Guilin—in geographic terms, the mountains are karst topography. This means the mountains began forming when that area of China was under water. As the seawater continued to recede, the salty water kept dissolving and eroding off the limestone layers, creating the beautiful mountains (which are actually stalagmites). There are so many beautiful sites around Guilin that I'll never forget—some include the beautiful Elephant Trunk Hill, Reed Flute Cave, and the many "cave" homes of Guilin residents living alongside the Li River. If you ever get an opportunity to visit China, make sure you go to Guilin and to the Great Wall of China, the only man-made place on Earth that Astronaut John Young said he could identify while piloting the space shuttle orbiting our planet.

Now back to Guilin's sister city gift to Orlando. On the east side of Lake Eola Park (diagonally across from the Black Marble) stands the beautiful red Chinese Ting (many call it a pagoda but Dr. Ying says the technical term is *ting*). Dr. Ying had suggested to Guilin's mayor, Zheng Yi, that Guilin's gift to Orlando should be a Chinese ting to be placed in Lake Eola Park, the most visible location in The City Beautiful and part of the city's great seal. The ting was constructed in Shanghai, disassembled, placed on another "slow boat from China," and delivered to the same Port of Jacksonville for processing through immigration.

Dr. Ying paid for five Chinese workers (none spoke English) to accompany the ting to Orlando. After I completed the immigration paperwork and the semi carrying the disassembled structure arrived at Lake Eola, the work to reconstruct the ting in the park began. Dr. Ying was in constant contact with the Chinese construction workers as they quickly assembled their bamboo scaffolding around the rising structure. If you have ever traveled to Hong Kong or any major city in China, you have seen Chinese construction workers effectively using bamboo scaffolding to bring structures out of the ground.

Several weeks into their work, OSHA (Occupational Safety and Health Administration) inspectors showed up and told the workers to stop—they placed a red Stop-Work Order on one of the bamboo poles, stating bamboo is unsafe and not legal for building scaffolding. Well, "What do you want me to do, Mayor?" I asked. He said, "Handle it, handle it—do whatever you have to do to get the ting up!" Does this remind you of a television show a few years ago, *Spin City?* I prayed and asked Jesus to give me the wisdom of Solomon to solve this problem.

The first thing I did was call our City Building Maintenance Department and ask the director to meet me down at Lake Eola. I shared with him the problem and asked that he have his workers come out and build a chain-link fence around the perimeter of the structure, put a lock on the entrance gate, and give me two keys—one for the construction foreman and one for me. Through our interpreter, I told the foreman not to allow anyone in the fence until the project was finished other than Dr. Ying or myself. I called my dear friend Tom Hunt, director of BellSouth Communications, and asked him to have his company lay a telephone wire from Eola Drive to the footprint of the ting construction. I asked him for a direct dial phone to Dr. Ying's office at EPCOT's China Pavilion, so that all the construction foreman had to do was pick up the phone and it automatically called Dr. Ying's office, where English translation could be conducted during construction.

By the end of the week, there were a number of red Stop-Work Orders placed on the fence. Please understand, I am *never* an advocate of disobeying the law; but when you have no other way to reconstruct a foreign structure, you must find another avenue to get the job done. In just a few short weeks, the ting was completed. God is so good!

Black Marble Stone at Lake Eola

Ting at Lake Eola

Ting Crew from Shanghai

Zheng Yi in Beijing's Great Hall

Zheng Yi in Beijing's Great Hall

Zheng Yi in Beijing's Great Hall

Li River in Guilin

Chapter 9

KEYS TO THE CITY

I will give you the keys of the kingdom of heaven.
—Matthew 16:19

During the Frederick administration, Walt Disney World offered to design a new VIP Key to the City of Orlando and the local newspaper ran a story on it. The keys were to be given out very selectively. Because we had so many types of keys designed by previous mayors, I kept them all in the old "gun vault safe" used by "Officer" Mayor Langford. Mayor Frederick told the reporter that I was the "keeper of the keys."

We had multiple types of keys varying in size and type of box or velvet drawstring bags for presentation. We had feminine type keys (in acrylic, like the presentation to Naomi and Wynonna Judd) and keys that could be hung on a necklace, standard cardboard box keys, and the beautiful, wooden carved boxes housing the twelve-inch key.

Often when the mayor was unavailable, he or she would delegate presentation requests to a commissioner or the mayor's chief of staff. Often, a VIP's representative would ask for their client to receive a key, and there were times key presentations were mayor/commission or staff initiated. The process was the same for proclamations, which seemed to be presented ten times as often as keys.

Mayor Langford's favorite recognition of an individual was to make him or her an "Honorary Orlando Police Officer," complete with a real badge, identification, and leather ID folder. Mayor Frederick continued this tradition but only for several years. It seems as though a couple of honorees (one from Langford and one from Frederick) abused the privilege and insisted the badge was an entitlement. Eventually, Mayor Frederick abolished the program forever, and I never discussed it when Mayor Hood was elected. I was always nervous about the potential for liability if nothing more than having a mayor's close friend ending up with a ticket or getting arrested depending on the degree of abuse.

I was blessed that Mayor Frederick trusted me with key to the city presentations. Perhaps the fondest memory was in 1984 when the mayor and Joanne were in France and Michael Jackson's entourage came to Church Street Station to dine at the elite Lili Marlene's Restaurant. Dick Milano, Bob Snow's general manager of Church Street Station, called me on a Saturday afternoon pleading for a key to be presented to Michael Jackson, who had just released his megapopular video, "Thriller." Keep in mind this was a time when this polite young man was super popular all over the world, had not yet toyed with cosmetic surgery, and seemed to me to be a pretty good kid. Dick said that Michael was a frequent visitor, loved The City Beautiful, and was considering buying a home here. He was accompanied by his mom and dad and the director of "Thriller," John Landis. Further, he said he would send a limo to my home to pick me up along with any members of my family. And, he would like for us to have dinner at Lili's as his guest. Well, I had a Boone High School fourteen-year-old daughter, Lori, who thought "Thriller" was the most wonderful video ever produced—she said she would be ready when the limo arrived. By the way, this thirteen-minute-forty-three-second video released on December 2, 1983 sold over 9 million units, and in 2009, "Thriller" became the very first video inducted into the National Film Registry of the Library of Congress.

Sure enough, at the stroke of six o'clock, the limo pulled into our Conway home driveway and Irma, Lori, and I were off to Church Street Station. It was always hard to keep Michael Jackson's visits to The City Beautiful quiet and that evening was no exception. Michael and his entourage had arrived a few minutes before six and were escorted through the back door of Rosie O'Grady's. When our limo arrived in front of 129 West Church Street, a large crowd was already milling in the street. When the limo driver opened the back door and out stepped this middle class family from North Carolina, there was a collective sigh mumbling, "Where's Michael?"

Michael Jackson was one of the most polite celebrities I've ever met. He was gracious at receiving the key and said, "Yes, sir" and "No, sir" to me and "No, ma'am" and "Yes, ma'am" to Irma and Lori. During dinner, the Jackson parents and Mr. Landis were down-to-earth folks and our time together was so enjoyable.

Over the years following our time with Michael Jackson, he aged with many struggles in life—financial mismanagement, parenting, etc.—and I always had a sorrow for him. Because of his popularity, he was not able to live the life of freedom we enjoy. His public life was a lot like Elvis Presley's. When Irma and I heard the news of Michael's death on June 25, 2009 (which was our forty-second wedding anniversary), newscasts were consumed with associated reports about his life. I recall for nearly a week after his passing the front page of our newspaper had numerous stories about local residents who had ever glimpsed the rock star (or knew someone who had) and I began to pray, "Lord, please don't let the media dig up the story of Michael Jackson getting a Key to the City of Orlando." The last half of Jackson's life was not as admirable as his early rock and roll days, and his popularity was very mixed. God answered my prayer.

Just a few other notable persons I was blessed to give keys to the city include legendary stock car racer Bobby Allison, 1983 NASCAR Champion and named one of NASCAR's top fifty drivers; our UNC-Chapel Hill Basketball Coach, Dean Smith—since Mayor Frederick went to Duke and I went to UNC, he graciously allowed me this honor; perhaps the greatest boxing champion of all time, Muhammad Ali; and seven-time NASCAR Stock Car Champion with two hundred victories, the King, Richard Petty.

Mayor Langford would always say when presenting a key to the city, "This key will not open any bank vaults, but it does open the hearts of our citizens to you."

Big Key to City

Smaller Keys to City

Richard Petty

Wynonna and Naomi Judd

Michael Jackson and Dick Milano

UNC Basketball Coach Dean Smith

Chapter 10

LETHAL WEAPON 3 AND MORE

*So whether you eat or drink or what-
ever you do, do it all for the glory of God.*

−1 CORINTHIANS 10:31

HERE IS AN AT&T U-verse commercial in which a preteen girl tells her even younger siblings how good they have it with modern day technology, saying, "In the old days we didn't have..." This older sister doesn't have a clue how good even she had it in her elementary school days.

When I began working in Mayor Langford's office, the city had not yet purchased its first computer/word processor. We used to type on triplicate carbons, and if you made a mistake you had to physically erase the typo with a pencil-like eraser with coarse, grey rubber as a tip on one end and a tiny brush on the other end to sweep off the error material.

As we moved through the 1980s, the city proceeded to put a computer on every city hall employee's desk. This technology became integrated with masses of wires and complex computer station rooms requiring special cooling and other mandates needed to produce efficient operation. It soon became apparent our old city hall could not physically keep up with advanced communications.

The Sunshine State has in its statutes the Florida Sunshine Law. This makes it illegal for members of the same board, agency, council, commission, or legislature—any group of elected or appointed officials—to discuss in private actions what may be voted on by that specific governmental entity. Since the mayor and commissioners could not discuss whether or not to build a new city hall unless they were in a previously posted meeting that would allow the attendance of the general public and press, it was my assignment as the mayor's chief of staff to "take the temperature" of the council and count the prospective votes for the mayor's agenda. We all had mixed emotions about getting rid of a building that had produced so much history and personal memories over the years. But the decision was a no-brainer if we were to have the necessary infrastructure for the future.

In 1992, the city entered into an agreement with the producers of the movie *Lethal Weapon 3* allowing them to use the implosion of the old city hall in the opening scene of their movie starring Mel Gibson and Danny Glover. Safely housed in our completed new city hall that stood only a few feet behind the old building, excitement was rampant as Hollywood began moving in sets and trailers for the stars. Mel Gibson was probably at the peak of his popularity and many women city hall employees were begging to meet him (so was my daughter, a sophomore at the University of Florida). Mayor Frederick suggested that I ask Mel if he would do a personnel tour of our building. He graciously agreed. When I met him at the door, he was smoking a cigarette. With as much country boy charm as I could muster, I said, "Mr. Gibson, I'm so sorry but our new city hall is a smoke free building." He responded sheepishly, "I understand, but I need for you to make an exception for me—I have to smoke!" Immediately, the proverbial question popped in my mind, "Where does an elephant sit? Anywhere he wants!" I got a large coffee cup and put a little water in it—during the tour, he handed me more than twenty butts, which I extinguished in the cup. No one seemed to mind!

Mayor Frederick confided in me that he would like to be in the movie with Mel and Danny. Oh, the assignments I have had over the years! I spoke with our liaison and the mayor's wish was granted. The mayor was given the role of the police captain rolling up to the scene of police detective partners, played by Mel Gibson and Danny Glover, running out of an exploding building. What really excited the mayor was the prospect of being a member of the Screen Actors Guild! When he found out only speaking roles qualified one for membership, the mayor's body seemed to droop. Since it was our building and all sorts of delays could have arisen, I guess, the producer wasted no time in giving the mayor a speaking role—one word: "Bravo!" At least he didn't have any lines to memorize, and all turned out well!

Unless one has experienced a movie scene production, the enormous amount of detail in preparing for perfection in triggering blasts timed exactly to the few seconds these two actors had to run out of the front of the old city hall is mind-boggling! Across the street from the front doors of 400 South Orange Avenue were stationed two giant jet engine fans used to blow the implosion dust back toward the crumbling building. This allowed the movie cameras to focus on the two actors so the movie patron could identify Mel and Danny as the humongous cloud of dust erupted at all 360 degrees.

The last day city employees were allowed to be in the old city hall, I took a photo out of the one north window in the mayor's office, capturing a last view up Orange Avenue. Soon thereafter, a large, glass "asparagus" would grow up out of the concrete jungle that is now part of the new city hall plaza (actually, it is a piece of art that used to light up at night and change colors).

The implosion was scheduled for no earlier than 7:00 p.m. on October 24, 1991, but because movie producers seemed to be in no hurry, the big boom did not take place until after midnight. There were thousands of people amassed to witness this piece of Orlando history. Even with the long delay in detonation, I do not recall any negligible reduction of onlookers. I remember coming in to work a couple of hours late the next morning expecting to find all of my office windows blown out. To this day, I stand amazed at the precision with which a demolition team can drop a structure in place. As I mentioned earlier, the new city hall sat less than fifteen feet behind the old building, and all the implosion did was twist one of the ground floor doors and blow out one window in my office (on the third floor). A new window had already been installed and had I not found a dime-sized shard of glass imbedded in my wall, I would not have seen any damage.

By the way, our daughter did come down from Gainesville, met Mel Gibson, and got several photos taken with him. Needless to say, she became the most popular member of the Chi Omega Sorority.

I must admit, meeting Mel Gibson and Danny Glover and discovering how down-to-earth they seemed to be reminds me of many other celebrities I've met who did not seem to have big egos. Some include actresses Delta Burke (former Miss Florida), Loni Anderson, and Carol Channing, and actors Ron Howard and Robert Wagner. However, an even bigger thrill came in 1996 when Orlando hosted World Cup Soccer. The USA women's team won gold medals, and Mayor Hood took me with her into the women's locker room after their final victory. I got my picture taken with the world's greatest soccer player of all time, Michelle Akers, a product of the University of Central Florida. I will forever cherish the many memories afforded me as a member of the different mayors' staffs. I am humbled and grateful.

Speaking of being humble and grateful for the opportunities to meet famous people, the real heroes in my life are the team of doctors God used to save my life time and time again. Over the last twenty-five years, approximately 175 doctors, surgeons, and oncologists have examined or treated me. Some of the key physicians include Klein Bowen, Wayne Jenkins, Clarence "Buck" Brown, Robert Faber, Julio Hajdenberg, Aurelio Duran, and my open-heart surgeon, Mark Sand. My Great Physician guided the minds and hands of these awesome docs and I feel so very blessed. Praise God from whom all blessings flow.

Mel Gibson

Mel Gibson and Lori James

City Hall Implosion

Filming of Lethal Weapon 3

Robert Wagner

Delta Burke

Michelle Akers

Carol Channing

Hello Dolly on Broadway with Carol Channing

Loni Anderson

Ron Howard and Mayor Frederick

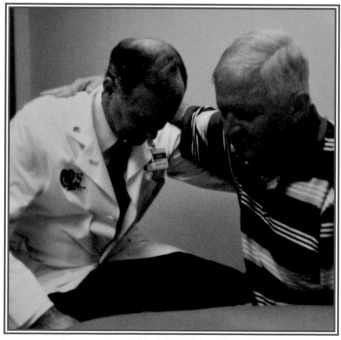

Praying with Dr. Mark Sand Before Heart Surgery

Last Photo from Old City Hall

Chapter 11

MAYOR GLENDA E. HOOD

Charm is deceptive, and beauty is fleeting; but a
woman who fears the LORD is to be praised.
—PROVERBS 31:30

EGARDING THE SCRIPTURE above, let me be right up front
in saying that Mayor Hood is a believer and "fears the Lord."
That is perhaps my greatest admiration for her during my
five years as her chief of staff! What a joy to be prayer partners with
the chief executive officer of the city of Orlando and to understand
that the wisdom to lead our wonderful city comes from above. The
greatest privilege she afforded me was asking me to pray for direc-
tion to make the right decisions. (Lest I forget to mention elsewhere
in the book, I was blessed, also, by the spiritual commitment displayed by Mayor Bill Frederick and Mayor Rich Crotty.)

Upon my retirement in 1997, Mayor Hood asked the Orlando
City Council to bestow upon me the title of Orlando Mayors' Chief
of Staff Emeritus—the signal recognition of my thirty-two years as
a government employee. I can never thank her enough!

Glenda Hood was sweet, kind, good natured, and skilled in nur-
turing great relationships with her constituents and peers. She was
faithful in her worship at St. Michael's Episcopal in College Park—I
had the privilege to accompany her to a few services and funerals
and witnessed how much the people adored her. I would describe
her as a devoted, meek leader. Lest any of her friends be offended by
my use of the word "meek," let me explain from a pastor's viewpoint:

you have seen beautiful stallions standing meekly and following the leadership of the reins. This is a true picture of "strength under control." In no way is the stallion any weaker because he is meek!

Neither in the ten years I served with Mayor Hood as she represented District 1 on our City Council, nor in the five years I was her mayoral chief of staff, did I ever see her "blow a fuse," treat anyone disrespectfully, or cry! At the beginning of her first term, I gave her some unsolicited advice: "Mayor, don't ever let the people see you cry! There will be some mean-spirited folks who will use that against you. I am being paid to be your number one whipping boy, and when you get angry and feel like exploding, call me in your office, shut the door, and cut loose!" A few weeks after her swearing in as Orlando's first woman mayor, she did exactly that. She called me in with all her authority, kicked the door shut (scared me just a little), and mildly yelled a question asking why one of our appointed officials could have done something so stupid! I was so proud of her—"strength under control!"

I have vivid memories of Glenda being very active in volunteerism. We called her "Glenda" whenever she visited Mayor Langford's office—since then, it was always "Commissioner" or "Mayor Hood." She served as vice-chair of the Municipal Planning Board and Zoning Commission. She was on the Nominating Board and was chair of the Task Force on Board and Commission Restructure.

Mayor Langford was very complimentary of Glenda, and every member of his office staff encouraged her to run for City Council. She was first elected in 1982.

Over my career in government and as a pastor at First Baptist Orlando, many have referred to me (my beautiful wife, Irma, included) as the "Energizer Bunny" because I have always had a tough time saying no to any request and "just kept on going." Mayor Hood had me beat hands down. I recall on several occasions we both exceeded one hundred hours of work in one week! At Christmastime, as was the custom of Mayor Langford and Mayor Frederick, Mayor Hood would hand each city employee his or her Christmas bonus check and shake each hand. No disrespect to the two previous mayors, but they both went to consolidated groups of employees to wish them Merry Christmas—it was just a logistical nightmare to meet with midnight shifts at police and fire headquarters and Orlando International Airport police substation. But not for Mayor Hood—"RJ, we are going to meet with every single city employee unless they are sick or on vacation."

As I was driving her home about one o'clock in the morning from meeting all midnight shifts, I reminded her I would be back at five o'clock so she could begin greeting dayshift police and fire squads. Dragging myself into her driveway at 4:55 a.m., I noticed it was pitch dark in her upstairs bedroom. I waited until 5:00 a.m. on the dot (Mayor Langford taught me to never be one minute late, Mayor Frederick often ran late, and Mayor Hood was in between) before calling her on my cell phone. It rang once, "I'll be right there!" I put the clock on her doubting we would be on time for the first OPD lineup at 5:15 a.m. She blew out that front door in five minutes flat, not a hair out of place, hopped in my car, and said, "Take my lipstick and keep it in your jacket pocket." Not another word was spoken by either of us until we pulled up to the police station back door to meet the watch commander at exactly the time she told him we would arrive. Whew! *Superwoman!*

Some of you more seasoned readers will know this paragraph may not seem to be politically correct—however, years back, political correctness was not as big of an issue in politics as it is today. I refer to the common terminology in the 1960s and 1970s as "the good old boys" and "smoke-filled back rooms." Each of the three Orlando mayors for whom I worked had his or her inner circle of advisers—just a sampling of Mayor Langford's opinion leaders included Egerton Van Den Berg, Henry Meiner, Norm "Booger Bear" Glass, Jim Robinson, and others. Mayor Frederick had more confidants including Jerry Chicone, Peter Barr, Reggie Moffitt, Jerry Billings, Jacob Stuart, Buddy McLin, and Dewey Burnsed, just to name a few.

Mayor Glenda was part of a feminine "power team"—out of respect for the mayor's sensitivity, I will not call it "the good old girls"—that produced an effective network of women leaders in Metro Orlando. Chairman of the Orange County Commission (later renamed by voters as Orange County Mayor) Linda Chapin governed the largest area of the county. Perhaps Mayor Hood's closest confidant was Dianna Morgan, Senior Vice President Human Resources and Public Affairs for Walt Disney's Community and Government Relations. Last, but certainly not least, was Jane Hames. Jane worked in public relations for many years and owned her own agency, Embassy Consultants. These four influential women were close friends (despite periodic political strains during Orlando's growth spurts and annexations), and every December for many years, they all traveled to New York City to do Christmas shopping and relax from the pressures of their individual responsibilities.

Florida Senator Toni Jennings (later appointed Lieutenant Governor by Governor Jeb Bush) was also a faithful confidante not only to the mayor but to me as well. She was an effective president of the Florida Senate and worked so well with Florida Speaker of the House Representative Dan Webster (now US Congressman Webster).

When God called me into full-time Christian ministry during the summer of 1997, I went in to tell the mayor I was retiring. She graciously offered me a very generous raise to stay; but when I declined and told her, "Jesus has called me," she immediately understood. She told me she wanted to host a retirement luncheon for me. I pleaded with her not to do that—I just wanted to slip out quietly after my last paycheck. Mayor Hood said, "We are going to have a luncheon and if you don't show up, you will be conspicuously absent!" There were eight hundred people (the maximum the Church Street Station Presidential Parlour Room would hold) who paid a steep price for lunch. Marla Weech, former Florida News Anchor of the Year, was the emcee and a number of prominent "roasters" kept the audience in stitches following the lead of Orlando Magic Senior VP Pat Williams. Orlando Chief of Police/Orange County Director of Public Safety/United States Marshal Thomas D. Hurlburt was chairman of the program.

I don't know how much they charged per person, but at the end of the event, Mayor Hood presented me a check for $25,000.00. I was so humbled but had the courage to tell the audience I was planning to use this money to buy our church school, The First Academy, their first big, new bus and would need an additional $17,000.00 in case anyone wanted to make additional donations after the program ended. Then God went to work on about a dozen donors who made up the balance. What a mighty God we serve!

Mayor Hood was elected three times as Orlando's mayor (1992, 1996, and 2000), but before completing her third term in 2003, she accepted Governor Jeb Bush's appointment as Florida's Secretary of State. Today, she is still active in volunteerism but mostly enjoys being with her husband, Charlie, as the two of them dote over their precious grandkids—something Irma and I look forward to doing with our grandkids very soon.

Mayor Hood and Chris Martin

News Anchor Marla Weech

Chapin, Morgan, Hood, and Hames

Mayor Hood Good-Bye Hug

Dr. Jay Strack and Lieutenant Governor Toni Jennings

Chapter 12

SMART WOMEN

You are a woman of noble character.
—RUTH 3:11B

E ARLIER, I SHARED with you about a period of Orlando history during which women dominated Orlando leadership: Orlando Mayor/Secretary of State Glenda Hood, Orange County Mayor Linda Chapin, Senate President/Lieutenant Governor Toni Jennings, and Disney Executive Vice President Dianna Morgan. However, many women of noble character have flown under the radar screen, often doing all the work for which their bosses may have received all the credit! That is definitely how it worked for all of us non-elected officials in local government. (Well, let me qualify that, since three of the four mayors I served are still alive and may read this: we did a *lot* of the work for them.)

Just another word on Mayor Hood. When Mayor Bill Frederick retired in 1992 and Mayor Hood moved into the executive suite of offices, a reporter asked me to compare how it was working for a woman after working for two male mayors. I told him that after moving out all of the trophies, autographed basketballs, footballs, and baseballs and moving in the vases, doilies, and pieces of art, there was no difference in my working relationship with our first female mayor. Mayor Hood had been well groomed during her ten years as a city commissioner and there could not have been a smoother transition. As mayor pro tem, she had experienced chairing council meetings and Mayor Frederick graciously allowed her to represent the city of Orlando in leadership positions with the Florida League of Cities and the National League of Cities. In just a few short years, this led to Commissioner Hood being elected as president of both of these prestigious associations before election to the mayor's office—the large majority of these offices were held by mayors. Commissioner Hood submitted a successful bid for Orlando to host the National League of Cities Congress and Exposition before she was elected mayor. This was a significant accomplishment that brought approximately ten thousand mayors, commissioners, and city managers to The City Beautiful.

Two of the significant women I was privileged to work alongside in the "city pressure cooker" were Grace Ann Chewning and Christine Martin. There were many other very successful women with whom I was honored to work—maybe I will write a sequel when I retire completely.

Right after the election of Orlando Mayor J. Rolfe Davis, Grace Ann Chewning graduated in 1953 from Boone High School, where she had become proficient in typing and short hand. At the tender young age of sixteen, she approached Orlando City Clerk Ed McDowell inquiring if he had a position for her—she is one of the most unintimidated women I know. After reviewing her qualifications and skills, he offered her a job as the cemetery clerk at a whopping salary of $35.00 per week! She did her job well and began climbing the ladder of success. Grace said she must have been desperate to go after the job and attempt to purchase her first car. At her age, no bank in Orlando would risk financing a car for her. So, as a member of the city family, she went to the city's credit union and promptly qualified to get her car. After being a faithful customer for ten years, Grace Chewning was elected to the board of directors at Orlando Federal Credit Union, was elected to every officer position, and still serves today.

In 1966, Grace married Bob Chewning—the two were together for forty years. When I was sworn in as an Orlando police officer, Bob Chewning had just been promoted from Orlando police chief to director of public safety. Director Chewning was the most handsome, debonair, "movie star looking," person I ever had as a boss—he was the spittin' image of Clark Gable! I will never forget one night walking into the squad room for line-up. Director Chewning happened by and the sergeant asked him if he would honor us with a troop inspection. This always brought back unpleasant memories of periodic surprise bunk, boot, weapon, and locker inspection when I was stationed at Lackland Air Force Base in San Antonio. A fiber of dust in the barrel of your service weapon always brought verbal wrath from the inspecting officer. Fortunately, Director Chewning was a compassionate professional and I had the utmost respect and admiration for him until the day the Lord took him home.

In 1976, Mayor Langford appointed Grace as Orlando City Clerk (the first female since 1875, and serving the longest at twenty-six years). In 2003 Grace received the Donald A. Cheney Award from the Orange County Regional History Center "in recognition of her outstanding efforts to champion and preserve the history of Orange County and Central Florida." Thank goodness she has some history preserved that will stay with only her! In 2008, the city dedicated "Chewning Way" at Greenwood Cemetery to honor both Chewnings for eighty years of combined dedicated service to the citizens of Orlando and Central Florida. This reminds me that every time I drove Mayor Langford (he never drove anywhere as mayor—he always had a staff person to chauffeur) passed Greenwood Cemetery, he would comment, "There lies the dead center of town!"

After forty-nine years of employment with the City of Orlando, Grace Ann Chewning retired with the City Council bestowing on her the well-earned title of Orlando City Clerk Emeritus. Still today, she has more knowledge of the city's history than any other person I know. And, I want to thank her publicly for assisting and supporting me through my career in the Orlando mayors' offices.

Christine Martin began working for the City of Orlando's Policies and Procedures Office in 1974 before making her way up to the city clerk's office. When Mayor Frederick came in my office and offered me the appointment as his chief of staff, I was very humbled yet bold enough to respond, "Yes, sir, if you will allow me to bring Chris Martin from the clerk's office to be my executive assistant." With one of his difficult to read facial expressions (a cross between

"I don't know" and "I'm glad I thought of that"), he replied, "Gracie is not going to be happy about it, but if you want her, go tell Gracie I said it was OK." At the end of his third term, I don't know who appreciated Chris more, the mayor or me!

When Mayor Frederick was elected in 1980, there were no computers in city hall. Word processors were new in the marketplace. In 1981, Jacob Stuart, Mayor Frederick's staff director, helped the city clerk's office get our first Wang computer. Jacob's dad, George Stuart, had one of the most well-known office supply stores in Orlando, and Jacob was a master of office equipment; he even taught me that my ballpoint pen was not a pen at all—it was a writing instrument. Please know I'm not making fun of Jacob, he is one of my very close friends and I love him like a brother; he has brought our Greater Orlando Chamber of Commerce positive, international recognition! But I do remember some stressful sessions between Chris and Jacob as they both fine-tuned their mastery of the Wang computer. I was as lost as a ball in high weeds when it came to that Wang; but oh, what a major step of progress from the Langford administration, when we typed on triplicate carbons and slipped doubled slips of paper behind each typo while we erased with those green pencils and gritty, pointed erasers with a little green brush on the other end to clean off the erasure debris.

Soon after Mayor Frederick and I saw the level of proficiency in word processing achieved by Chris Martin, we both purchased little recorders (just a tad bigger than most iPods) and dictated memos, letters, reports, speeches, and so forth. Chris used her transcriber to produce the documents with amazing speed. Mayor Frederick was a very articulate visionary with a vocabulary beyond anyone I knew. One of his directives to me was to proofread any document placed in his signature file. Believe me, this was labor intensive. However, Chris' vocabulary blossomed as she had to look up strange words she heard on his recorder. Then, when I did my proofreading, I would stick my head around the corner and ask her what some of those strange words meant. Chris began to assist me with budgets, minutes, and every hard task in our administration. She knew my mind well enough to prepare many letters of response before I had a chance to read the initial constituent inquiry. Her abilities aided me in accomplishing more each year.

When Mayor Frederick decided not to run for a fourth term, Mayor Hood asked Chris and me to lead her new staff. I stayed five years as Mayor Hood's chief of staff before the Lord called me into full time ministry. When I retired, I asked Chris to come on staff with me at First Baptist. She declined because of the commitment she had made to Mayor Hood to stay through her second four-year term (she had two years of commitment left). At the end of Mayor Hood's second term, I went back to Chris with an offer and asked her to go home and discuss it with her husband. The next day, she accepted. Chris worked with me a number of years, serving our First Orlando Foundation and our finance office.

Chris was also a talented communicator to the deaf. While working in the mayor's office, the Orlando Police Department called her to go atop a building on Orange Avenue, where a deaf man was threatening to jump. Chris responded immediately and talked the man down using her skills in sign language. She received an award of merit from the OPD. She signs for the deaf in many services in her church.

Chris Martin and her husband, Rick, are two of the godliest people I know. Surely there will be many crowns in heaven for them both.

"In conclusion" (one of Mayor Langford's favorite opening comments when giving welcomes to visiting conventions), the photo with Grace Chewning standing directly behind the 55 Speed Limit sign with Mayor Frederick and Chris Martin to her immediate left was taken at Mayor Frederick's fifty-fifth birthday party thrown by all of our appointed officials. At the party, the mayor asked me why the staff had such large name tags around their necks. I blamed Grace and Chris saying maybe these name tags will be large enough for him to read without his glasses (at many city functions using name tags, he usually reminded me he wanted the first names in large, bold print with the last names smaller and underneath the first names in case he might have left his glasses in the car). Anyway, we all had fun, and the mayor was a good sport about it!

Shaq with Chris Martin

Frederick's 55th Birthday

Chapter 13

PAYNE STEWART'S
LEGACY LIVES

When I consider your heavens, the work of your fin-
gers, the moon and the stars, which you have set in
place, what is man that you are mindful of him?

−Psalm 8:3–4

I was blessed to have been one of Payne Stewart's disciplers the last six months of his life. I helped him understand a broader meaning of various scriptures and the basic disciplines to best encourage development of spiritual maturity. I had come to know Payne and Tracey through their two precious children, Chelsea and Aaron—our daughter, Lori, taught Aaron in the seventh grade.

It was Payne and Tracey's curiosity with the transformation of their children's hearts that caused them to make a closer inspection of what their two children were being taught at our school, The First Academy (TFA). This was about the same time Orel Hershiser had been inviting Payne to our church to visit a men's Bible study led by Orel. Ironically, Orel and his wife, Jamie, liked the education their two sons, Quinton and Jordan, were receiving at TFA (Lori also taught Jordan in the seventh grade). Orel graciously did some promo videos from the TFA mound of Hershiser Field—named after "Bulldog," one of the Los Angeles Dodgers' great pitchers. I believe God used Orel to help Payne grow in his faith.

Payne called me in April '99 and asked that I show him the architectural renderings of our proposed TFA athletic fields. He suggested

I give him the names of twelve couples I felt might be interested in helping fund the project. Payne said, "You give me their names and phone numbers and I'll personally call and invite them to my home for a barbeque and I'll do the cooking. After we eat, you bring out the drawings and tell us how much it will cost!" Payne was pumped! He continued, "Randall, after you state the cost, I'm going to say, 'OK, friends, Tracey and I are going to give a half million dollars for construction—how much will you give?'" Because of Payne's and Tracey's willingness to step forward and trust God to use them to prompt others to give, we received a $1.2 million commitment. They were a generous giving couple!

Payne Stewart is the only person I could identify from his backside (as could most every golf fan) as he was walking hundreds of yards down the fairway. Who could ever forget his infamous knickerbockers/patterned pants and his ivy-style caps? One day, he took me into his closet area and let me see his cool wardrobe!

I will never forget having breakfast with Payne and Tracey at Le Peep near the intersection of Kirkman and Conroy. I asked Payne if he realized he had overachieved in marriage. Tracey is a very private, soft-spoken, beautiful woman and she has an air of elegance—especially when her Australian accent graces every word out of her mouth. She reminds me of Princess Diana. Tracey was so very kind to the First Orlando Foundation (she served on my FOF board for several years), and to this day I pray for her often.

It seems only a few Sunday afternoons ago that I was glued to the front of our television watching the US Open in Pinehurst, located in the southern area of my home state of North Carolina. Payne had won the 1991 US Open in a sudden death playoff and I was praying so hard he could win again in 1999. I had left Payne a voice mail on his cell phone mid-week encouraging him and reminding him of Philippians 4:13 (NKJV), "I can do all things through Christ who strengthens me." As he and Phil Mickelson battled on the last tournament hole, Payne had a fifteen-foot putt for par that would give him the win—it was riveting TV! When Payne's ball disappeared in the eighteenth hole, I let out a blood-curdling yell! When I thought this was the peak of excitement for that afternoon, I again had cold chills during the victory interview when Payne held up his arm and pointed out his WWJD bracelet (What Would Jesus Do) given to him by his son, Aaron, and gave God the glory for his victory!

Right after Payne Stewart's exciting victory at the 1999 US Open, he brought me the yellow flag from the eighteenth hole and autographed it in my office (so I was a witness). That December at the Payne Stewart Memorial Celebrity Tournament Dinner Auction benefitting the TFA sports complex, the eighteenth hole flag sold for $31,000.00!

On October 15, 1999, just ten days before Payne Stewart soared in a private jet to meet Jesus in the air, our First Orlando Foundation (FOF) honored Payne with our beautiful Crystal Eagle Legacy Award for his bold leadership in helping to make famous the name of Jesus. The event was a fundraising dinner auction benefitting our First Center for Pregnancy. Then Orlando mayor Glenda Hood honored Payne with a key to the city and gave a proclamation declaring October 15 Payne Stewart Day in Orlando. However, the highlight of the night for me was watching Payne's emotions build as three single moms with their small children in tow followed one another to the microphone and gave their testimony. Each admitted they had made some poor choices in life, and out of desperation, each of these expectant women turned to our pregnancy center for help. They were welcomed with open, loving arms by our counselors and volunteers, and without a hint of judgment they were offered free sonograms. Each woman shared that when she saw the tiny image of her baby and heard the heartbeat, all three knew abortion was not the solution. Our center provides a way for moms to earn food, clothing, Pampers, cribs, toys, and so forth; and, more importantly, we strive to help them restore their dignity. Additionally, our center does post-abortion counseling with the love of Jesus, and provides many social services usually provided by Orange County.

As Payne approached the lectern to receive his Crystal Eagle, many witnessed monster tears streaming down both of his cheeks. His first words at the mike: "These moms should be the honorees tonight instead of me—they are the real heroes!" The evidence of Payne's newfound faith was so obvious on that very special night.

On October 25, 1999, a Learjet flying from Orlando to Dallas was carrying Payne Stewart and two other friends of mine, Robert Fraley and Van Ardan, along with well-known golf course designer Bruce Borland, and the two pilots when it crashed into a field near Mina, South Dakota. It was reported that all six on board were believers in Jesus Christ.

The memorial service for Payne was held at 11:00 a.m. in our worship center. I recall counting forty-seven television trucks with satellite masts parked in a reserved lot next to the church. In order to lessen the appearance of a media circus, which surely would have added stress to Tracey, Chelsea, and Aaron Stewart, we disallowed any cameras in the worship center other than our own used for our weekly services, and provided our satellite dish hookup to every media outlet on our property. The service was broadcast live without interruption on a half dozen cable networks including ESPN, CNN, and the Golf Channel. Tracey approved of our foundation printing this statement on the programs and videos of the service: "The Stewart Family has requested proceeds and gifts in Payne's honor to go to The First Orlando Foundation, 3000 South John Young Parkway, Orlando, Florida 32805-6691."

In the days, weeks, and months following the service, over one hundred thousand dollars poured in from around the world to memorialize one of golf's most beloved and well-known champions. Every penny donated in Payne's honor was invested in building the Payne Stewart Athletic Complex (PSAC) located at our back entrance off John Young Parkway. Most of the gifts were accompanied by sympathy notes to the family and comments of how Payne's service had brought them to faith or restored their faith.

I am not able to adequately articulate the appropriate thanks due Tracey and Payne Stewart for their investment in the lives of many thousands of young athletes using this state-of-the-art facility. I told

Tracey that Payne's life and death had a positive impact on more people's faith than if God had let him live to be eighty-five.

Today, the Payne Stewart Athletic Complex hosts high school football, baseball, softball, and multiple state and regional track and field events. It is the home of the Golden South Classic, where men and women Olympic track hopefuls have registered Olympic qualifying times. PSAC serves as a practice facility for college football teams invited to Orlando bowl events and for Major League Baseball spring tryouts. Thank You, Lord, for allowing us to have Payne for a season.

Orel Hershiser and Mark O'Meara

Payne Stewart Athletic Complex – Track

Don and Irene Dizney with Payne Stewart

Payne Stewart Athletic Complex – Football Field

Payne Stewart and the James Family

Payne Stewart Memorial Service

Chapter 14

CHILDREN'S CHILDREN

Children's children are a crown to the aged.

–Proverbs 17:6

D URING MY QUARTER of a century working for the City of
Orlando, I was blessed with numerous opportunities to
meet many celebrities, other VIPs, and six different presi-
dents of the United States. "Lord, who am I that You are mindful
of me?" (Ps. 8:4) However, there is a price associated with so many
activities—long days, long weeks, and long years. I missed a lot of
personal family time as our daughter, Lori, grew up while her dad
was at work. I must stop right now and thank my beautiful wife,
Irma, for the wonderful way in which she helped raise our only child
while I was away so much (e.g., three successful trade missions to
Asia during two different administrations).

However, I serve a mighty God of second chances...He gave me
a much more manageable schedule following the births of our two
precious grandchildren, Chase and Hayley. I so enjoyed just "sucking
their little ears off" as they, too, have grown up before my very eyes
(both are now teenagers and I'm sure when they are reading this line,
they are both cringing). "Sucking their little ears off" is a North
Carolina country boy translation for "loving them as much as I pos-
sibly could." You can take the boy out of the country, but you can't
take the country out of the boy—please remember this as you read
some of my other descriptions throughout this book.

Chase began kindergarten at The First Academy—our awesome

Christian K–12 school with approximately twelve hundred students, a ministry of FBC/O—not long after I completed my service in Mayor Rich Crotty's Office. I was an "executive on loan" from the church to Orange County to relocate each member of Mayor Mel Martinez's staff and appoint a new staff for Mayor Crotty. Chase was a little intimidated in his first year even though his mother was a seventh grade TFA history teacher and my office was in sight of his classroom. The first few months of class, I made it a point to be in the lunchroom every day when Mrs. Dinah Callahan's class marched in for 11:25 a.m. lunch. It brought Chase joy when I would sit beside him at lunch as he got to better know his classmates.

The afternoon after I got the invitation to ride with the president of the United States from the airport to the Orange County Convention Center, I asked Chase what he thought about me missing lunch with him. He never looked up when he said, "But Granddaddy, you always have lunch with me!" Immediately I replied, "Son, you know I am *not* going to miss having lunch with you!" He gave my right leg such a tight hug that I knew I had made the right decision.

I must admit I was a little bit surprised when David Ettinger, editor of our monthly in-house publication, *The Spirit,* called me and wanted to do a "paragraph or two" on the invite from the White House. He interviewed me for about fifteen minutes, and in a couple of weeks, the publication came out with a full page spread with two color photos—one of President George W. Bush at the presidential podium and the other of my family and President George H. W. Bush when he was attending a 2006 Fall Festival at our church. The headline: "Snubbing the President? Say It Ain't So!" To say the least, I was besieged by calls and e-mails from many of my coworkers asking, "Are you crazy?" The reporter ended the story with my comment, "You know, after that day, I never did hear from President Bush again." But that's quite OK—the honorable Jeb Bush wrote the Foreword of this book!

My fellow pastor friend and renowned leadership author John Maxwell's quote, "People don't care how much you know until they know how much you care" is very applicable in this life lesson! My grandson had no idea I had to make a decision about having lunch with him or riding with President Bush—I always had lunch with him and he trusted my faithfulness. However, I suspect when he becomes an adult, he may better realize the depth of my love for him! A word to parents who have young children: it is better to do things with them and make memories than to give many material things (Game Boys, PlayStations, iPods, etc.) that will be short lived. I remember nearly every vacation and trip we took as a family when I was a kid, and the only two gifts I can remember are a bicycle and tiny transistor radio with one earplug.

Earlier in this chapter, I mentioned Mayor Rich Crotty and the trust he placed in me to be his first chief of staff. And, speaking of children, one of the most memorable stories of the Crotty administration is about his son, Tyler. Some of you may remember from the local news and/or the David Letterman show about Mayor Crotty taking Tyler to hear President George W. Bush speak. The event was held at the Orange County Convention Center and Tyler was conspicuously standing on the stage right behind President Bush. The speech was rather long and young Tyler soon became bored and uninterested. The cameras caught him several times as he yawned, stretched, and looked at his watch. It was even more hilarious because President Bush did not have a clue the world was watching Tyler rather than him. Soon, David Letterman had Tyler as one of his guests on *The Late Show* and he showed news clips over and over. It was side-splitting funny.

On a more personal note, the next summer Mayor Crotty told me Tyler had asked Jesus to be the Lord of his life and he wanted me to baptize him on the beach of Lake Conway. They invited neighbors to celebrate with Tyler and it was my joy to baptize him.

Make memories with your kids—they will be grown and gone before you know it!

TYLER CROTTY ON DAVID LETTERMAN - MARCH, 2004

Tyler Crotty and David Letterman

Tyler Crotty Baptism in Lake Conway

President Bush and James Family

Chapter 15

VISIONARY EXTRAORDINAIRE: JIM ROBINSON

A good name is more desirable than great riches;
to be esteemed is better than silver or gold.

—PROVERBS 22:1

O NE OF THE most humbling things Mayor Langford used to do to me (or for me, depending on the group) was including my introduction at welcomes to conventions and associations meeting in the greater Orlando area. Nearly always he would introduce me as the person who does all the work for which he "gets all the credit." There is a lot of truth in that statement not only for me but for appointed officials and senior staff.

Perhaps the one public servant who had the greatest overall impact on the history of Metro Orlando may surprise you. Why don't I stop right here—without scanning your eyes to the next paragraph, who do you Orlando history buffs think he or she might be? Keep in mind that the answer I give is just my humble opinion.

In 1948, Jim Robinson, having served in World War II in France and Germany and having returned to the University of Florida to finish law school, was admitted to practice law in Florida. After almost sixty-five years of service and at the age of ninety, he still drives himself to the office of Giles and Robinson five days a week. Leon Handley calls him "the Dean of the Orange County Bar." I don't know any other attorney who has been practicing law that long. His practice now consists of almost all pro bono work.

I could sit all day and listen to Jim tell stories of life nearly a century ago. Jim told me about his experience with ROTC at the University of Florida, where he was assigned to the artillery division. At that time, training was performed with horse-drawn artillery. Those "caissons went rolling along." Teams of horses pulled the caissons and the French 75s (quick-firing field artillery pieces adopted in 1898 widely regarded as the first modern artillery pieces used in World War I). When the Military Ball and parade were held each year, the horses would bolt and run until stopped by the fence at the end of the parade ground. Officers rode individual horses, and the first-year privates rode on the caissons. After Jim's second year, the horse-drawn artillery was replaced by trucks and World War II 105mm howitzers. I'm certainly not calling my dear friend "old," but he goes way back!

Jim was appointed Orange County attorney in 1958. He served through most of the 1960s, a time when Orange County was rapidly changing from a rural to an urban community. He negotiated with the representatives and attorneys of the Walt Disney Company and I have seen him depicted in a video of the Walt Disney Company in the archives of Disney's historical footage.

In the 1960s, a group of public-spirited people led by Senator Beth Johnson (the park next to the Greater Orlando Chamber of Commerce is named in her honor), Bill Dial, Martin Andersen, Henry Land, Jim Robinson, and others saw the need to secure a new state university for east Central Florida. There was some opposition from other state universities and alumni of those schools. They saw a further diversion of limited funds available for state universities. The Central Florida Development Committee led the effort to get legislation passed and support for a new university.

After legislation was adopted, suggested sites were offered. The Board of Control deadlocked three to three on Sanford Airport and South Orange Blossom Trail sites. Jim Robinson suggested a former ranch on Alafaya Trail then owned by Frank Adamucci, a developer from New Jersey. The site was selected. There were no funds available for purchase or costs and no legal authority to obtain them. Jim Robinson spearheaded a group of about ninety people who signed promissory notes producing almost one million dollars. It took four years for Orange County to get legislation approved and to levy taxes and relieve the ninety people of their obligations. A list of these people, called the founders, is on a plaque in the welcome center at the University of Central Florida (UCF).

Frank Adamucci, at Jim's request, gave up to five hundred acres free and received $1,000.00 per acre for the same number of acreage. Martin Andersen, publisher of the *Orlando Sentinel*, was quoted by Ormond Powers: "Robinson never did get credit for what he did." Well, he did get credit about twenty-eight years after the event, in 1992. Dr. Charles Millican, President Emeritus of UCF, issued a resolution of the founders citing Jim Robinson as "Visionary Extraordinaire" and second UCF President, Dr. Trevor Colburn, who did a study of the founding of the university, introduced Jim saying, "If anyone could be called the Father of UCF it would be Jim Robinson." Raymer Maguire Jr., a founder of Valencia College, said "Every time I think of UCF, I thank Jim Robinson. Without him, we wouldn't have it."

UCF awarded Jim an honorary degree, "Doctor of Public Service," in 1989. During my service in Mayor Langford's and Mayor Frederick's offices, God blessed me with the favor of Dr. Millican, Dr. Colburn, and Raymer Maguire Jr., three very gifted leaders in Orlando's history.

In the mid-1970s, Jim Robinson was appointed attorney for the newly created Greater Orlando Aviation Authority (GOAA). The federal government turned the McCoy Airport over to the city of Orlando largely due to the efforts of Mayor Carl Langford. The Authority was composed of public-minded people such as City Commissioner Wally Sanderlin, chairman; Harry Bower, CPA; Sherman Dantzler, president of the First F.A.; I am honored to have called all three of these men my friends. Some were elected for two years and some for four years. The city had no funds to construct runways and an international terminal. Jim Robinson negotiated agreements with the four airlines, which provided that the airlines would guarantee the payment of bonds so cost of construction could be accomplished without the use of local tax money. The agreement was for thirty years and became standard for airport and airline use. I'm not sure many people realize what a feat this was for the future of the greatest airport in the world (once again, my humble opinion). I am super proud of Orlando International Airport today and the exciting plans GOAA and Phil Brown, executive director, and his team have on the drawing board.

During the time between 1976 and 1980, Champ Williams held an exclusive franchise for the sale of all kinds of food at the airport. Champ wanted a thirty-year extension of his contract without bidding. It was during this time (which was the first four years of my twenty-five years of serving in the mayor's office) that I got to know Jim Robinson well. During the final months of negotiations between Mayor Langford and Mr. Williams regarding specific details of the extension request, there were several times that the mayor and I met in Mr. William's Skyline Restaurant office. Both men wanted a witness to discussions (which later caused me a lengthy appearance before the grand jury); Langford chose me and Champ chose his son, Stephen Williams, to sit at the table.

Finally, the time came when neither principal could come to agreement. Mayor Langford followed Mr. Robinson's counsel and the Skyline sued us. Jim Robinson advised the authorities it violated the agreement with the airlines and he could not approve it. The Authority members changed and fired Jim and approved the extension. The Authority had the right to fire its attorney if he would not agree to support what it was doing. Delta Airlines (represented by now Senior United States District Judge Greg Presnell) sued the Authority, and Federal Judge George Young issued a ruling that upheld the advice given by Jim Robinson. In the ensuing uproar, public opinion resulted in a restructuring of the Authority, and current members were replaced. The power of appointing of the membership was removed from the City of Orlando by the state legislature and given to the governor of Florida—today, I still strongly feel these appointments should be made by the Orlando mayor and City Council. As it stands today, the City of Orlando owns the airport, subject to some federal government provisions, but does not select the members of the Authority who operate it.

In May 2012, Chairman Frank Kruppenbacher, on behalf of the Greater Orlando Aviation Authority, awarded Jim Robinson with a resolution honoring him for his time served as attorney during the early years.

Jim Robinson also served Central Florida and his country in many other ways: president of the Chamber of Commerce; president of Orlando Kiwanis Club; president of Children's Home Society; president of Channel 24 PBS Television; elder and Sunday school teacher of First Presbyterian Church of Orlando; secretary of the Presbyterian Retirement Communities (now Westminster Retirement Communities); member, Permanent Judicial Commission Presbyterian Church US; member, Board of World Missions Presbyterian Church US; and member of the Foundation Presbyterian Church US. There are many other instances of his service in our community. If you think about it, did Jim Robinson not have a major impact on the history of Orlando?

In 1985, Jim assisted Irma and me in establishing financing for our new home, which was built within the city limits of Orlando. Pressure from several City Council members insisting the mayor's chief of staff should live in the city made the decision necessary—and it was right that we live in the city I represented. I never regretted the move nor did I take offense at the wisdom of those commissioners.

I remind Jim often that he overachieved in marriage. Jim and Betty were high school sweethearts. He was president of the class of 1940 at Orlando High School and Betty was class secretary. They were both elected most likely to succeed by their classmates. Jim and Betty are among our dearest friends, and I thank God for arranging our paths to intersect.

Jim Robinson

Chapter 16

MOVERS AND SHAKERS

A cord of three strands is not easily broken.
–ECCLESIASTES 4:12, HCSB

REFLECTING ON THE metamorphosis of this once sleepy little community first known as Jernigan in the mid-1800s, we must realize we stand today on the shoulders of many great men and women who worked hard to build the foundation on which stands The City Beautiful. Almost immediately after the City of Orlando employed me in 1974, I began to learn about the origins of street names and other venues named in honor of those responsible for their existence.

Then, as my responsibilities broadened in the mayor's office, I began building relationships with so many people who were at that time beginning to have a positive effect on the quality of life for our citizens. I have already mentioned many of those "movers and shakers" in preceding chapters, but many others are indelibly etched in my memory. When one begins listing leaders, there is a real risk of unintentionally leaving out the names of many other noteworthy influencers. Therefore, I will randomly mention a non-exclusive sampling of those I recall making a positive difference.

Corb Sarchet was a soft-spoken man who Mayor Langford appointed to the Library Board, and later became the first director of the Downtown Development Board. Corb was a leader in the Boy Scouts for over fifty-five years and was seen proudly wearing his scout uniform at least once a week. But what I remember and love best about him was his desire to create an arts and crafts event at Lake Eola. I recall him coming in to get Mayor Langford's blessing, and in 1978, the very first Fiesta in the Park was deemed a success. Today, the event draws large crowds to enjoy the work of over six hundred artists, crafts, and fabulous food.

Jerry Chicone, Jr. is one of the most respected names in the Florida citrus industry and was elected to the Florida Citrus Hall of Fame. Jerry and his sweet wife, Sue, were always so kind to me as I often battled cancer. Jerry played a very active leadership role as president of the Orlando Chamber of Commerce and the Orlando Utilities Commission and as chairman of the Downtown Development Board. He would call my office at least a couple of times a month and suggest a situation needed attention; e.g., "On the southeast corner of so and so, the pocket park has a lot of weeds—let's keep Orlando beautiful!" I never minded his calls because they were all "for the good of Orlando." However, one of the most important but little known good deeds Jerry did for Mayor Frederick happened as we were implementing our Conserv II project. The court had ordered the city to cease pumping effluent (our treated wastewater was clean enough to drink) into Lake Toho via Shingle Creek, "headwaters of the Everglades." Mayor Frederick's project called for spreading the treated water over the citrus groves of west Orange County, and Jerry led the way in convincing enough other citrus owners to accommodate the flow. Conserv 11 won many national and international awards thanks in part to Jerry and his influence on fellow citrus growers.

J. Charles Gray has served his community well. He is the founding director of the GrayRobinson Law Firm (every attribute I note about Mr. Gray was founded before Gene Shipley, my son-in-law, became a partner in his firm) and is one of the finest gentlemen I have ever known. Just a few of his leadership positions include chairman of the Florida State Turnpike Authority and the Economic Development Commission of Mid-Florida, University of Central Florida Trustee Emeritus, and recipient of a very long list of community service awards. He and his wife, Saundra, have sailed completely around the earth. From my personal involvement, I felt most thankful for the seven years Charlie was the Orange County attorney. There is an old country song that talks about the city always fighting the county and vice versa. In all my years of working in government, there were often times of friction and fussing in every administration. Charlie Gray was the epitome of a peacemaker and I witnessed his calming influence numerous times as he was the "glue" that held together various city-county issues.

Rick Fletcher is a lawyer and business owner who always reminded me of one of the Beach Boys with his tanned good looks, handsome smile, and his semi-shaggy curls resting on his shirt collar. Rick looks "cool" to this very day! He served as president of the Orlando Utilities Commission, the Downtown Development Board, and the University Club. Rick has served as chairman of our First Baptist Orlando Board of Trustees and he and his beautiful wife, Suzanne, are founders of our church's First Life Crisis Pregnancy Center. Rick's passion, though, has been the recent establishment of the Grace Medical Home (GMH) located in downtown Orlando. Led by Dr. Marvin Hardy Jr. and his team of doctors and staff, GMH provides healthcare to those who do not have insurance and cannot afford medical services. This is an awesome ministry that pleases God!

Colonel Joe Kittinger and Commander John Young are Orlando's two greatest space heroes. God gave me favor with both. John Young has been launched into space more than any other human in history. Joe Kittinger was the first human in space (not Soviet Yuri Gagarin in 1961). On August 16, 1960, Col. Joe jumped from a military test balloon from more than nineteen miles up in space—102,800 feet— his free-falling body broke the sound barrier. He spent nearly one year as a prisoner of war in Vietnam. But I will always remember Joe and his wife, Sherry, for the kindness they showed Irma and me when I was going through a very difficult time of harsh chemotherapy for lung cancer. I have never smoked in my life, but my oncologist feels I contracted lung cancer from my dad through passive smoking. During this valley in my life, three couples "ministered" to me. Bob and Linda Snow (founders of Church Street Station) provided an aircraft for Joe and Sherry to fly Irma and me to the Bahamas for a week's stay on a beautiful yacht provided by Mayor Bill and Joanne Frederick. My oncologist told me the exact day my hair would fall out from the chemo and he was accurate. God used these six folks to minimize my stress of going bald.

There are many men and women responsible for building the Orlando International Airport, arguably the finest airport in the world. Just a few of the notables with whom I had the pleasure to work include Mayor Carl Langford, John Wyckoff, Jim Robinson, Norman Glass, Egerton Van Den Berg, Mayor Bill Frederick, Mayor Linda Chapin, Sherman Dantzler, Jeff Fuqua, Carolyn Fennell, Bill Jennings, and today's executive director, Phil Brown. There were many others, but these are effective leaders I witnessed firsthand develop the "economic engine" that drives our local economy.

In the early 1990s, at a program at Howard Junior High School, Mayor Glenda Hood introduced me to the school's outgoing and personable principal, Ronald Blocker. I knew instantly his star would be rising soon. Ron served as an effective Orange County school superintendent for twelve years (despite several critical editorials from the local paper). Most of all, I admired Ron's faith and felt blessed when he would e-mail me to pray over certain issues to improve Orange County's schools.

In my humble opinion, the Millennia Mall would not exist today if it were not for the tireless efforts of Schrimsher Properties, Inc. One of the more complex, intricate infrastructure requirements required to bring the mall project to fruition was the construction of the Interstate 4 interchange at Conroy Road. This one project opened my eyes to the reality of bureaucratic "red tape" more than most. Papa Joe, Steve, Frank, and Mike Schrimsher persevered and never gave up, praise God!

When it comes to "clean industry," figuratively and literally, two corporations led the way: Campus Crusade for Christ and Wycliffe Bible Translators. In 1989, Dr. Bill and Vonette Bright announced their decision to move the international headquarters of Campus Crusade from California to Orlando. Campus Crusade is one of the largest ministries in the world, and Bill and Vonette have greatly enriched my spiritual life over the years. Bob and Dallas Creson are effectively leading Wycliffe Bible Translators, a ministry where translators are now working on more than 1,500 different languages. The Cresons, also, have been wonderful Christian friends. Orlando is blessed to be the home of both of these wonderful organizations.

The arts community is a vital component in creating a vibrant community sought out by Fortune 500 companies when considering corporate headquarters locations. Orlando has been well served for forty-two years by the director of the Orlando Museum of Art, Marena Grant Morrisey. She has been instrumental in bringing a wealth of exciting shows and exhibitions to The City Beautiful, but my favorite was the 1997 "Imperial Tombs of China" exhibition. Having been on several Asian trade missions and enjoying the opportunity to see the actual terra cotta horsemen in Xian, China, my memories were even more three dimensional. Marena is a kind, soft-spoken professional I will never forget.

Apopka's mayor, the Honorable John Land, is the longest serving full-time mayor in the United States. He was first elected in 1949, and still serves in that capacity today. I am humbled to have been voted as a lifetime member of the Tri-County League of Cities (Orange, Seminole, and Osceola counties) and I owe Mayor Land for his support of this distinction. There are many reasons why the citizens of Apopka have reelected him as their chief executive officer so many times.

Serving as Mayor Bill Frederick's chief of staff in the 1980s when Pat Williams asked for an appointment to discuss with the mayor the possibility of bringing the National Basketball Association to Orlando brings back memories of several God-sized miracles. First, we didn't have a facility for a team to call home—that didn't stop Pat! The old adage, "build it and they will come," seemed too great a risk—but not for Pat, Mayor Frederick, or Jim Hewitt. Because of their heroic efforts, Orlando has been the beneficiary of many philanthropic blessings from Rich and Helen DeVos. Go Magic!

Mayor Langford introduced me to State Representative Dick Batchelor in 1977 and a long-lasting friendship began. Even when we were not on the same political page, we found it easy to disagree without being disagreeable. I thought I had served on a lot of committees, boards, and commissions over the past thirty-five years, but I can't come close to matching Dick. Today, his "Dick Batchelor Run for the Children" has raised well over one million dollars and he has been recognized with many child advocacy awards. However, to me, the most endearing of Dick's attributes is his thoughtfulness and encouragement to me through my many years of fighting cancer. "A friend in need is a friend indeed!"

From July 19, 1963 until November 27, 1964, Colonel Stanley I. Hand served as Commander, 306th Bomb Wing at McCoy Air Force Base in Orlando. Even since his retirement, Colonel Hand has been a respected leader and counselor in our community. I think of Colonel Hand each time I pass by the B-52 Memorial Park alongside the main entrance into the Orlando International Airport. I wonder how many folks in our community are hearing about this awesome park for the first time; google it and then take your children and grandchildren—mine were amazed at the size of this retired B-52D Stratofortress, so large that the tips of the wings have wheels. Colonel Stan and Marjorie Hand are among our dearest friends.

This would be a good segue into another story about one of my military heroes. In the early 1980s I met a member of the Tangerine Sports Commission (the name of the annual game was changed in 1983 to the Florida Citrus Bowl game), Alex Marsh—known as AM to his close friends. AM is an Orlando businessman who is ninety years young and still drives to work every day. While lettering in high school in football, basketball, baseball, and track, Alex had aspirations of being a professional baseball player for the Detroit Tigers, but a farming accident left him with a debilitating injury to his arm. On December 16, 1944, while serving his country in the European Theater of Operations on the Belgium-German border, AM's 106th Infantry Division was captured by the Germans in the Battle of the Bulge. He was a prisoner of war (POW), and lost over forty pounds in the next three-plus months, but recalls one of the happiest days of his life when on April 1, 1945, General George Patton's Tank Corps rolled in and freed every POW. I thank God for living in a country that believes in fighting for freedom. We should always honor the men and women of our armed forces and never forget their service and sacrifice to make our nation great.

One last mover and shaker whom I would like to thank for helping me learn the ropes of leading a nonprofit foundation is John Bozard. John and I have both been members of First Baptist Orlando for more than a quarter of a century. While I worked in the Orlando mayor's office, he and I both served on the church's personnel committee—we both had terms as chairman. A brilliant financial analyst, John was gracious to assist me in performing an industry standard pay scale adjustment for church employees—John made me look smart. When I retired from the city and joined the church staff, I barely knew what a foundation was—again, John helped me look like I knew what I was doing, and I will be forever grateful. Moreover, John's selfless efforts and leadership on community boards and committees have truly helped make Orlando wonderful.

Lastly, I want to thank Orange County Mayor Teresa Jacobs for her friendship and support since her first campaign in 2000, when she was elected to the first of two four-year terms on the commission before becoming Orange County Mayor. When I was appointed by Chief Judge Belvin Perry to serve on the Orange County Task Force for Ethics and Campaign Finance Reform, Teresa was a "bulldog advisor" with tremendous wisdom to share with the task force. I felt underqualified serving with this prominent team of Orange County movers and shakers: Mayor Linda Chapin (Chair), Scott Gabrielson (Vice-Chair), Alvin Cowans, Terri Day, Jose Fajardo, Frank Kruppenbacher, and myself. Many of Teresa's ideas were integrated in our final recommendation. Just this week, I have completed serving on jury duty and voting in our local, state, and national elections—what a privilege! Living in the greatest nation in the world demands we faithfully participate in our civic duties and I encourage everyone to be a part of the processes that keep our country free.

LINDA CHAPIN

ALVIN J. COWANS

OC Task Force for Ethics and Campaign Finance Reform

Mayor Teresa Jacobs

Mayor Frederick and Norm Glass

Ron Blocker

Colonel Joe Kittinger

John Bozard and Arnold Palmer

Colonel Stan and Marjorie Hand

Pat Williams' Granddaughter Laila Kindy

2012 Fall Festival at Lake Eola

Chapter 17

TINKER FIELD HOSTED
TWO YANKEE GREATS

As iron sharpens iron, so one man sharpens another.
—PROVERBS 27:17

OR MANY YEARS, I had the privilege of serving on two great committees: The Mayors' Prayer Breakfast committee and the Sea World Easter Sunrise Service committee. Both gave me the opportunity to become personally acquainted with men and women known across this nation for their leadership, courage, bravery, and commitment to Christ. A few names included Rich DeVos (owner of the Orlando Magic), Truett Cathy (founder of Chick-fil-A), Colonel Oliver North (decorated marine and political commentator), Dr. Billy Graham (internationally known evangelist), Don Beebe (wide receiver for Super Bowl Champion Green Bay Packers), Danny Wuerffel (Florida Gators quarterback and Heisman Trophy winner), Michelle Akers (National Soccer Hall of Fame), Bobby Bowden (Florida State head football coach), Fred Grandy (from *The Love Boat* television series), John Schneider (from *The Dukes of Hazzard* television series), Orel Hershiser (Dodgers pitcher Hall of Famer), and Bobby Richardson (record-holding Yankees second baseman).

Since I was in first grade, Bobby Richardson and Mickey Mantle have been my two favorite New York Yankees ever! Both of these superstars have played before Orlando fans at Tinker Field. Mayor Langford gave me a Mickey Mantle autographed baseball. But nothing excited me more than serving as chair of the twenty-third

Sea World Easter Sunrise Service Special Guests Committee. It was my responsibility to call Bobby Richardson at his home in Sumter, South Carolina, and invite him to be our keynote speaker on April 3, 1999. For those of you not familiar with Bobby's accomplishments as a Yankee, he was a seven-time All Star, five-time Gold Glover, and 1960 World Series MVP (Most Valuable Player)—the only World Series MVP on a losing team. Bobby and Mickey were great friends during their MLB careers and beyond.

As for Mickey Charles Mantle, my guess is that many non-fans of Major League Baseball know a little about the achievements of this great Yankee centerfielder. Legendary Yankees manager Casey Stengel said about Mantle, "He owns the smartest set of muscles I ever saw." Mickey hit 536 homers in his 18 years in New York pin-stripes, and many were tape-measure shots. He won seven World Championship rings and three MVP awards before being inducted into the Hall of Fame. His career was cut short by chronic pain from many leg injuries. Mickey partied hard during and after his career, and in 1994 he turned to the Betty Ford Center, where he was able to defeat the bottle.

In June of 1995, oncologists confirmed cancer had destroyed "the Mick's" liver. He was blessed to receive a transplant, which gave hope to all of his fans. But not long afterward, doctors discovered the cancer had spread elsewhere in his body—chemo and radiation could not stop the spread. Mickey knew in his heart he did not have long to live. From his deathbed in Texas, Mickey called on his longtime friend Bobby Richardson. It was what happened in the following weeks that prompted me to invite Bobby to our Easter Sunrise Service to tell "The Real Mickey Mantle Story."

When I called Bobby, he said without hesitation that he would be honored to come to share his testimony. Then he said, "Randall, would you be kind enough to get rooms and Sea World admissions for my grandkids when I come to Orlando?" I said, "Of course! How many grandkids do you have?" With a proud tone (that I understand firsthand about grandkids), he answered, "Thirteen!" "Deal," I said with excitement, having just talked in person to one of my heroes!

Bobby Richardson gave a wonderful eulogy at Mantle's service on August 15, 1995 at Lover's Lane Methodist Church in Dallas. Thousands heard Bobby tell how he knew he would see Mickey again one day. To my knowledge, since television was invented there are only two athletes' funerals that have been televised on ESPN live without interruption: Mickey Mantle's, and golfer Payne Stewart's.

Recently, I tracked down Bobby and asked his permission to use some of his quotes from Mickey's service. He said yes on the phone and followed up with a kind note containing his approval and thanks for writing the book. The note, along with one of the Mickey Mantle testimony tracts I've been passing out for years, was tucked inside of the Bobby Richardson Authorized Pictorial Magazine— what an awesome publication!

As I pondered Bobby's permission and the funny stories, I decided to share his entire eulogy as was broadcast live on international television...here goes, from the heart of Bobby Richardson:

I want to make a transition now from crying and sadness to laughter because if you know Mickey, he was always laughing.

And he enjoyed playing football in the back yard with the boys.

He enjoyed golf games at Preston Trails with the boys, and their traveling to autograph sessions with him.

But the teammates that are here today will also know that he always kept all of us laughing.

I remember the Mongoose in Detroit in the clubhouse.

I remember the snake that he put in Marshall Bridge's uniform in Kansas City before he was dressing that day.

He always ran out of money and he borrowed money from Yogi and Yogi would charge him 50% no, that's not in there.

I'm sorry...I take that back Yogi...

Yogi flew in today on Bob Hope's plane and he's flying out tomorrow with President Ford's plane.

But Yogi was a manager in 1964.

The Yankees lost four games in a row in Chicago.

Tony Kubek had brought some harmonicas.

He gave one to Phil Lintz.

Phil didn't play in any of those ballgames but on the bus, with Yogi in the front, he chose this time to learn how to play his harmonica.

Well, he played for a while and Yogi took as much as he could and finally he jumped up and he said, "Put that thing in your pocket!"

He didn't use those words but something to that effect and Phil was in the back of the bus and he didn't hear what he said and he said, "What did he say?"

And Mickey was sitting over across the aisle and whispered back, "He said he couldn't hear you. Play it again!"

And Yogi was the manager in '64 when Whitey Ford and Mickey started talking about how good they were in other sports, basketball in particular.

And it ended up, we played the cadets at West Point.

Whitey was to have the pitchers and catchers and Mickey was to have the infielders and outfielders and there would be a great game at the gymnasium at West Point after the regulars got out of the lineup.

Well, Yogi said, "Somebody's gonna get hurt."

Well, Mickey did it right.

He had uniforms for his players, he had a limousine, he had a chauffeur.

He did like this, and they took players on Mickey's team over to the game and came back.

And it was a great game.

Mickey's team won!

Tommy Tresh was voted most valuable.

Yogi was right…Steve Hamilton, the only one that played professional basketball, turned his ankle, and he was hurt.

But you know so many good things that Mickey did that people never heard about.

I remember that he flew across the country for Fritz Packel when he was dying with cancer.

In this church, right here, he did a benefit for Missions Outreach.

And over the years, he very seldom said no.

He came to my hometown on numerous occasions but in particular for the YMCA.

We had a great banquet.

There was a highlights film.

And then we went out to the ballpark and Mickey was to give a batting exhibition.

Something you just can't imagine him doing.

Tony Kubek was there.

Tony throws straight over handed, same speed all the time.

He was chosen to pitch to Mickey.

Everything was all set but Tony changed up on Mickey on the first pitch, and he swung and missed and pulled his leg and if he could have run he would have chased Tony around the field.

Tony made up for it though.

He (Mickey) hit one in the light towers in right field in the old-timers game that followed that.

But underneath all of Mickey's laughter and kindness there was a fear of death and an emptiness that he tried to cover and fill, sometimes with harmful choices.

Remember Bob (Costas) when he said on his interview, "There's still an emptiness inside."

The last game Mickey and I played together was on October 2nd, 1966.

It was in Chicago and we were at the Bismarck Hotel.

And I had invited a friend, a friend of mine, a friend of Mickey's to come over and speak to the ball club.

His name was Billy Zeoli, president of Gospel Films.

I remember standing in the back of the room that

was set aside and most of the players were there in attendance.

And looking over their shoulders at the fine, efficient, professional baseball players were there.

And yet I knew that all of us had problems.

Some financial... Some marital... Problems of various natures...

And yet my friend, that day, gave the answer to each one of these problems in the person of Jesus Christ.

He held his Bible up and said, "The Bible says three things.

1) The Bible says there is a problem and the problem is sin

2) The Bible gives the answer to the problem in the Person of Jesus Christ and

3) The Bible demands a decision."

And then he turned around and he had a blackboard and a piece of chalk and he wrote this question up on the blackboard, "What have you done with Jesus Christ?"

And then he went on to give three possible answers.

Number one was to say "yes," to accept Jesus Christ as Lord and Savior.

And I remember looking around that room at some of my teammates that I knew had said "yes" to Christ.

The second possibility was to say "no."

And I knew there were some of us that were unwilling to give up, perhaps, what we had going at the time.

And the third possibility was to say "maybe," to put it off to a more convenient time with good intentions.

But my friend made this statement.

He said saying "maybe," because of the "X" factor of death, automatically puts you in the "no" category.

I didn't really understand that then, but some years later, not too many years ago, we had a reunion of the 1961 New York Yankees in Atlantic City NJ.

The players were there in attendance.

It was a wonderful time of thinking back and remembering.

But in my room that night, I realized that three were not there.

Roger Maris, who broke Babe Ruth's home run record and a battle with cancer.

Elston Howard, that fine catcher on the ball club with a heart condition.

And a young pitcher by the name of Duke Maas.

And so I understood what he meant when he said, "Because of the 'X' factor of death, it's really "no."

So really only two choices, one to say 'yes,' the other "no."

And then my big thrill in baseball when a young teammate of mine who played for the next seven or eight years came up and said, "You know, I've never heard that before, a personal relationship with a living Savior that gives to us abundant life.

I would like to receive Jesus Christ as my Savior."

And that's the excitement but there's more excitement.

I came here to Dallas during the All-Star break this past month.

Mickey Mantle and Whitey Ford and I serve on the BAT board and I was here because of that.

And I had gotten the number from Whitey and I called Mickey and we had a great conversation.

And then the next morning, about six o'clock, he called my room and Betsy answered the phone and he said, "Betsy, is Bobby there? I would like for him to pray for me."

And we had a wonderful time on the telephone that morning, praying and I remember that I used the verse of Scripture.

I said, "Mickey, there's a great verse in Philippians 4. It says, 'delight yourself in the Lord.

Find your joy in Him at all times. Never forget His nearness.'

And then it says, 'tell God, in details, your problems, your anxieties.

And the promises of peace of God which passeth all understanding shall keep our hearts and minds as we rest in Christ Jesus.'"

We talked two or three more times and I went back to South Carolina and I received a call from Roy True, his friend and lawyer, and he said, "Mickey's not doing very well and the family would like for you to consider the possibility of coming out and being in the service."

And I asked Merlyn if it would be alright if I could come on out and she said, "yes."

Well, I came on in, I guess it was last Wednesday night.

Friends picked me up at the airport and I spent the night with them, it was late.

And the next morning, I drove over to Baylor Hospital.

Whitey Ford was just walking out at the time and Mickey had really perked up with Whitey's visit.

And as I walked in and over to his bed, he had that smile on his face.

And he looked at me and the first thing he said was, "Bobby, I've been wanting to tell you something.

I want you to know I have received Christ as my Savior."

Well, I cried a little bit, I'm sure, and we had prayer together and then in a very simple way I said, "Mickey, I just want to make sure!" and I went over God's plan of salvation with him.

That God loved us and had a plan, a purpose and a plan for all of us and sent His Son, the Lord Jesus Christ, to shed His precious blood and promise in His word that if we repent of our sins and receive the Lord

Jesus that we might not only have everlasting life but the joy of letting Him live His life in us.

He said, 'That's what I've done."

Well, the big three came in that afternoon.

That's Moose Skowron and Hank Bauer and Johnny Blanchard.

And they had a wonderful visit again with Mickey.

My wife and I came back later that afternoon and I remember that Mickey was in bed but wanted to be in the reclining chair.

And David and Danny and a couple of others I think helped him over.

He was laughing then.

When David grabbed him, he said, "Do you want to dance?"

But he sat in the chair and my wife, Betsy, sat down by him and shared her testimony.

And then she asked him a question.

She said, "Mickey, if God were here today and you were standing before Him and He would ask the question, 'Why should I let you in My heaven?' what would you say?"

As quick as a flash, he said, "For God so loved the world He gave His only begotten Son and whosoever believeth in Him should not perish but have everlasting life."

Well, I guess it was a little bit later and I said, "Mickey, you remember your day in New York?

You had heard me use a little poem called 'God's Hall of Fame.'

You talked about using it that day."

He said, "Yea, I should have."

I said, "No. I'm not sure that was the right time Mickey."

But you know, I think it is the right time today.

It says it all.

It says,

"Your name may not appear down here
In this world's Hall of Fame.
In fact, you may be so unknown
That no one knows your name;

The headlines may pass you by,
The neon lights of blue,
But if you love and serve the Lord,
Then I have great news for you.

This Hall of Fame is only good
As long as time shall be;
But keep in mind, God's Hall of Fame
Is for eternity.

This crowd on earth they soon forget
The heroes of the past.
They cheer like mad until you fail
And that's how long you last.
But in God's Hall of Fame
By just believing on His Son
Inscribed you'll find your name.

I tell you, friend, I wouldn't trade
My name, however small,
That's written there beyond the stars
In that Celestial Hall,
For any famous name on earth,
Or glory that it shares;
I'd rather be an unknown here
And have my name up there."[2]

---

2   Author unknown

Mickey's last press conference, he once again mentions his struggle with alcohol and a desire to be a dad to his boys.

He also mentioned his real heroes, the organ donors.

I hope you will all support the Mickey Mantle Foundation that addresses these issues and join his team.

But, if Mick could hold a press conference where he is today, I know that he would introduce you to his real Hero.

The One Who died in his place to give him not just a longer physical life but everlasting life, his Savior, Jesus Christ.

And the greatest tribute you could give to Mickey today would be for you to receive his Savior too.

Let's bow for prayer.

Thank you God that You loved us so much that You gave Your only Son Who willingly came and died for our sins, according to Scriptures.

And then He was buried and rose again on the third day, according to the Scriptures.

May each of us today honestly answer the question, "What have I done with Jesus?"

I'm so glad that someone shared with me years ago and perhaps you would like to pray as I did then.

God, thank You for loving me and sending Your Son to shed His precious blood and right now, I'm sorry for my sin.

And I receive You as Lord and Savior.

Thank You for coming into my heart.

To God be the glory

—BOBBY RICHARDSON
AUGUST 15, 1995

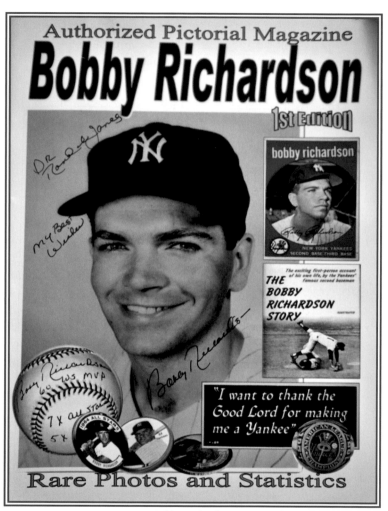

Bobby Richardson

Mickey Mantle and Bobby Richardson

Mickey Mantle Testimony Tract

Chapter 18

TWELVE MINUTES
FROM ETERNITY

*"You will be my witnesses in Jerusalem, and in all
Judea and Samaria, and to the ends of the earth."*
−ACTS 1:8

A   S I COME to the end of this book in which I have tried
to give you a first-person perspective from behind
the political scenes, I want to share with you a brief firsthand view backstage of serving the Lord in His house. I have three
passions in my full-time ministry: 1) sharing the good news of the
gospel to those God sends across my path; 2) administering the
two ordinances originated by our heavenly Father—baptism and
the Lord's Supper; and 3) giving of my time and resources to those
in need of encouragement and assistance—this runs the gamut
of preaching funerals, loving on cancer patients and their families, and providing financial assistance not only upon request but
anonymously, just to mention a few. Teaching "Developing Spiritual
Maturity" in our church for many years, I stressed that our goal in
life is to be more like Jesus—the two best ways are when we serve
and when we forgive. Jesus said in Matthew 20:28, "[I] did not come
to be served, but to serve…" We are told in 1 Corinthians 13:5 that
true love "keeps no record of wrongs."

I have preached many funerals over the years, several before I
entered full time ministry, including services for Ocoee Mayor Bill
Breeze and Orlando Chief Building Official Bill Neese. God gave

me the opportunity to tell both of these men what Jesus had done for them before they stepped into eternity and I look forward to seeing them both again one day.

In his book *Just As I Am,* Dr. Billy Graham recalls the 1963 National Prayer Breakfast, where he and President John Kennedy, our nation's thirty-fifth president, both spoke on the program. Privately, Kennedy had inquired of Dr. Graham about biblical concerns and about the second coming of Jesus. As the two men walked side by side out of the hotel to the presidential limo, Kennedy asked Dr. Graham if he had time to ride with him back to the White House to discuss those issues. Graham told the president that he had the flu and fever, and did not want to get him sick. Dr. Graham asked for a rain check to come visit the president later. In just a few short weeks, on November 22, 1963, President Kennedy was shot and killed in Dallas. Billy Graham calls his missed visit with the president "an irrecoverable moment."

My frequent prayer is, "Lord, please don't allow me to have irrecoverable moments." I nearly allowed one of those moments to happen several years ago. When our senior pastor, Dr. David Uth, gave the invitation to anyone needing to make a decision, he encouraged them to come forward and speak to one of our pastors standing in front of the altar. As the congregation sang the last verse, I saw one of our men who served in a church leadership position walking with purpose directly to me. Never losing eye contact as he neared, my mind was asking, "What kind of decision could he be coming to make?" He hugged me tightly and told me his mother was dying and she refused to listen to any question about her faith. In fact, she would raise her hand in the face of anyone speaking the name of Jesus. My friend and his wife had been trying to share the gospel with her for twenty years, but to no avail. He asked if I would come to his house and speak with her. I asked if she would live until Tuesday, as my Monday was booked from dawn to dark. "I don't know!" he replied.

Lying in bed that Sunday night, I told Irma about the matter. Immediately, she asked, "What are you going to do if she dies tomorrow?" I didn't even answer and rolled over to pray myself to sleep. Many times the Holy Spirit speaks to me through my wife, and I knew right then He wanted me to go see Miss Margaret the next morning.

When I walked into Miss Margaret's bedroom, the hospice nurse was holding her hand—I could see she was unresponsive and in a coma. I asked how long she had been like that. The nurse said, "All night; and she is going to die any moment." I asked the nurse to allow me to slip up on the side of the bed so I could speak in her ear. "Miss Margaret, my name is Randall James and Jesus sent me here this morning to tell you how much He loves you and how He wants you to love Him back."

She opened her eyes and stared compassionately into my eyes. I held her hand and asked her to squeeze my hand if she knew what I was saying. She gave me a weak squeeze but it was as thrilling to me as if she had yelled, "Yes!" I told her it was as easy as ABC to give her heart to Jesus and I asked her if she would like to do that right now. She squeezed my hand and smiled a little sweeter. I instructed her to pray silently in her heart, repeating my words only if she meant every word. "Understand?" I asked. She squeezed even harder. After I finished my prayer and said amen, I asked her if she had asked Jesus to forgive her and come into her heart to be the Lord of her life. One final squeeze from Miss Margaret and my heart was jumping for joy! As I slid off the bed, I told her I would see her in heaven soon. As I turned to hug Margaret's son, the nurse said, "Turn around, Pastor James. She is holding both arms up and wants to give you a hug." I hugged her gently, kissed her forehead, and left for the church.

I was driving back to my office and had been gone only about twelve minutes when my cell phone rang and my friend said, "Mom just passed away." My very first response was, "Thank You, Jesus!" But after further reflection, I said to myself, "This precious sister was only twelve minutes from hell!" Miss Margaret was proof that you are never too late or too old to ask Jesus to take control of your life.

I'm reminded of another who came to Christ before it was too late. Judge Bob Wattles was battling cancer when his sweet wife, Patricia Strowbridge, asked me to share my faith with him. I had some quality time with him alone in his home when he asked Jesus into his heart—just a few days before Jesus took him to heaven. Chief Judge Belvin Perry joined me in conducting a wonderful celebration service honoring the life of Judge Wattles.

Because of many years of cancer treatments and my continued survival, I've become known to many as the Cancer Pastor at First Baptist. One day, the church received a call from a woman who watched our services on television and wanted to speak with the Cancer Pastor. Her oncologist told her that she would be dying soon from her cancer and she wanted to be baptized. The problem was, she was bald from chemo and did not want to be baptized in front of others. I scheduled Debbie to come in on a Thursday afternoon and assured her the water would be warm but the worship center would be empty and very dimly lit. She asked if she could bring her two best friends, and I advised her she could bring as many of her friends as she would like.

When they arrived, I asked another of our pastors, Dr. Ragan Vandegriff, and a couple of our women staff members to join us in the baptismal counseling area. I shared the good news of Christ to all three, and even though Debbie was the one who had first asked for baptism, she and her two best friends prayed to invite Jesus to be Lord of their lives, and I baptized all three of them. We are always prepared to share the gospel and to baptize right then and there because, as Pastor David told our folks recently, "If you didn't bring your 'stuff' to be baptized, we have all the 'stuff' you need—shorts, shirts, robes for men, women, and children! So don't let 'stuff' hold you back!" It was probably the greatest celebration we've ever had on a Thursday afternoon.

But that is not the end of Debbie's story. Several weeks later, I received a call from one of Debbie's friends whom I baptized that afternoon. She said Debbie was in MD Anderson Cancer Hospital and her health was declining fast, and she asked if I could come right then. I put down what I was doing and rushed to the hospital.

When I walked in the room, Debbie was lying there with two IVs in her arms and looking so weak. When she saw me, she jumped up out of the bed to give me a hug—my heart nearly stopped! "Please lie back down before you pull something loose!" I told her. She told me she was not afraid to die, but asked if I would pray for her cancer to go into remission. On the way down the hall to her room, I saw one of the nurses from our church, who I knew loved Jesus. I asked her if she would join me in prayer. I anointed Debbie with oil (according to James 5:14), laid one of my hands on her head and, with the other hand holding Debbie's hand and the nurse's hand, we prayed to Jehovah Rophe, our Great Physician, to heal Debbie. After the nurse prayed as well, we both sang a chorus of "Thank You, Jesus." There was an immediate stillness and a feeling of peace in the room.

Several days later, I had to leave for Nashville to chair our quarterly meeting of the Southern Baptist Convention's executive committee. When I returned to my office the following week, I had such an accumulation of mail, e-mails, and phone messages that I did not follow up on Debbie. About a month later, I got an e-mail from Debbie (I have saved it to this day) saying her hair was growing back nicely and her oncologist had just given her an all clear—she was cancer free! After praising Jesus with her on the phone, I told her that if I ever wrote a book, I'd love to share her story. Without hesitation, she said, "I want you to tell the story—and use the pictures of my bald head if you wish." As Paul Harvey would say, "Now you know the rest of the story." What a mighty God we serve!

Matthew and Emily Mars

Debbie Simpkins' Baptism

EPILOGUE

I have fought the good fought, I have fin-
ished the race, I have kept the faith.
—2 TIMOTHY 4:7

OW THAT EACH chapter is complete, I ponder whether or not I have included something unique to each reader. There are so many untold stories that I could fill a half dozen volumes each the size of *War and Peace*. This prompts the question, "Should I write another book(s)?" If I had to give a firm answer this morning, it would be a resounding, "No!" I just told Irma that if I ever say I'm going to write another book, "Just haul off and slap me as hard as you can!" Writing a book is hard; but if there is a next book, I will do as the Holy Spirit assigns me.

When Mayor Frederick called me into his office one morning and said, "Shut the door and sit down," I knew I was in for a teachable moment. He had identified a couple of typos in his signature file. "From now on, Randall," he said, his firm voice rolling out a new staff ordinance, "I don't want anyone other than you placing any signature file on my desk. Then, if there is a typo or incorrect information, I won't have to track down but one person!" That occurred over thirty years ago, and ever since, I have striven to be a diligent proofreader and confirmer of information. I applied this same discipline in this book, but I have never had a college English instructor review my every jot and tittle. Thank you, Pat Birkhead, for making me look smart…the operative word is "look."

I want to thank my employers in Orlando who have given me a multitude of opportunities to make a difference in this great city.

Orlando police chief Jim Goode took a risk by relying on the recommendation of a mutual friend when he hired me on the spot (that was a "God thing" and doesn't happen in large departments today). Mayor Carl T. Langford did due diligence on me via a year's observation of how I conducted myself as sergeant-at-arms for Orlando City Council meetings. Mayor Bill Frederick relied on the evaluations given me by his close advisors. Mayor Glenda E. Hood made her decision to appoint me as her first chief of staff based on our ten-year working relationship when she served as an Orlando city commissioner. Dr. Jim Henry acted on impressions from the Holy Spirit that I should join his leadership team at First Baptist Church of Orlando—and he made it happen. Orange County Mayor Rich Crotty, a personal friend for more than twenty-five years and a member of my church, asked Dr. Henry if he could "borrow" me for six months to hire and organize his new staff—Brother Jim said yes, and continued my church salary as a gift to the citizens of Orange County. Finally, when Dr. David Uth was voted on by the church to replace our redeployed Pastor Emeritus, Jim Henry, Pastor David gave me the opportunity to serve on his strategy team. I thank each of them, and I thank God.

Due to space constrictions, there were so many exciting and memorable occasions not mentioned in other chapters. Just a few include taking my wife and grandkids on a tour of the United States Capitol with Senator Mel Martinez; taking Mikhail Baryshnikov to an Orlando Magic basketball game; having lunch with Prime Minister Margaret Thatcher; negotiating with Dr. Charles Stanley the sale of SBC's television network to In Touch television; photographing the top of my grandson Chase's head as Tim Tebow autographed his football; and sitting on the front row beside Franklin Graham at Dr. Bill Bright's memorial service in our worship center.

After much worldwide travel and admitting my personal prejudice, I am convinced Orlando is one of the finest metropolitan areas in the entire world. There are many contributing factors: great weather year-round (the "Sunshine State"); incorrupt civic and governmental leadership; a very diverse population; Orlando's new Medical City at Lake Nona, complementing already stellar hospital communities;

the epitome of year-round entertainment options for tourists as well as locals; a technologically advanced international airport; a state-of-the-art venue for the NBA's Orlando Magic basketball team; one of the coolest major performing arts centers (nearing completion); and many other unique features. I want to thank Mayor Dyer for his leadership in building our new Amway Center, the Dr. Phillips Performing Arts Center, SunRail, and for appointing Paul Rooney as Orlando's police chief.

In closing, I want to acknowledge that I feel I am the richest man on Earth—not financially, but because of the many times God has spared my life (I have undergone forty-five surgeries just for cancer). Just a year ago, my heart gave out and my aortic valve was replaced with bovine tissue. Today, my heart works like a Swiss clock—but every time I drive past a Chick-fil-A, my steering wheel nudges toward the restaurant. Thank You, Lord, for using Dr. Aurelio Duran and Dr. Mark Sand.

By far, my greatest joy is having the assurance of my salvation through faith in the atoning blood of my Lord and Savior Jesus Christ. My prayer is that every reader will experience this same joy before it is too late.

TNT's Craig Sager

Prime Minister Margaret Thatcher

Dr. Jim Henry with the Jameses

Dr. Rick Warren, Dr. Jim Henry, and Dr. Jay Strack

Senator Mel Martinez with the James Family

Mikhail Baryshnikov at Orlando Magic NBA Game

Tim Tebow Signing Chase's Football

Dr. David and Rachel Uth

Dr. Charles Stanley of FBC Atlanta

ABOUT THE AUTHOR

PASTOR RANDALL JAMES and his wife, Irma, along with their kids and grandkids live in Orlando, Florida, and serve as ambassadors for Jesus Christ. After more than fifteen years of serving on the staff of First Baptist Church of Orlando, senior pastor Dr. David Uth and the personnel committee designated Pastor James as President Emeritus of the First Orlando Foundation. He asked to be redeployed to volunteering in pastoral care so that he and Irma might enjoy more time together.

CONTACT THE AUTHOR

The author may be reached by e-mail at rljwilson46@gmail.com.

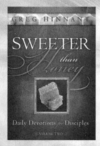